HUMAN TRAFFICKING

Law Enforcement
Reference Guide

Jennifer Fisher

Human Trafficking: Law Enforcement Resource Guide

Jennifer Fisher

ISBN: 1442175362
EAN-13   978-1-4421-7536-5

Published by Coastal Books, Supply, North Carolina,
May 11, 2009.

Photographs taken from the United States Department of
State, 2006 and 2007 Trafficking in Persons Reports.

Contact Information:
Coastal Books, cagney364@yahoo.com.

Printed in the United States of America.

Dedication

I would like to dedicate this book to all the past, present and future victims of slavery.

I would also like to dedicate this book to my husband, Jonathan D. Fisher, and my two sons, Isaih D. Fisher and Jacob A. Fisher, as well as my mother, Christy Judah for her inspiration and motivation.

Thank You

I would like to say thank you to, Christy Judah, for helping me during the development of this book. Without her, this book would not have been possible. I would also like to thank all of the individuals who supported me during this process.

Table of Contents

Introduction

"He has sent me to bind up the broken hearted, to proclaim freedom for the captives and release from darkness for the prisoners..." Isaiah 61:1

Human trafficking is one of the single most prominent civil rights violations occurring in modern times. The study and attention given to human trafficking is equivalent to what was given to domestic violence thirty years ago. Many people are shocked to find that human trafficking occurs in their own community.

With the influx of illegal immigrants into our country, this crime is being masked through other behaviors and businesses. Federal sex trafficking cases have increased each year since 2000, which is when the sex trafficking law was first enacted. A recent study by the National Institute of Justice, found that, in general, most law enforcement personnel, prosecutors, and service providers lack the ability to identify human trafficking, list the elements of human trafficking, differentiate human trafficking from human smuggling, and distinguish between domestic and international human trafficking. The same study established a communication gap between local law enforcement personnel and victim service agencies. These deficits are now being recognized and addressed by law enforcement communities across the nation.

Presently, in 2009, there are an estimated 30 million victims of human trafficking in the world. It is projected that there will be one million new victims of human trafficking each year. (Trafficking In Person Report 2008)

As these figures become more staggering, it becomes necessary for the law enforcement agencies to share information with field personnel and community agencies in order to understand and enforce the newly formulated laws and regulations.

This book was designed to provide an introduction for the law enforcement community, participating agencies that support the victims, and the general public to become more informed about human trafficking in the United States. It is my hope that this work will enlighten all citizens and help to stop the crime against the natural and life-earned rights of freedom entitled to each and every human being.

Jennifer H. B. Fisher, M. S

Chapter 1

Human Trafficking in the United States

"Neither slavery nor involuntary servitude, except as punishment for crime whereof the party shall have been duly convicted, shall exist within the United States, nor any place subject to their jurisdiction."

-13th Amendment to the United States Constitution, December 6, 1865.

History of Slavery

Slavery began to flourish in America beginning in 1619 when both white and African slaves were imported into Virginia. In 1807 laws were being written to abolish the importation of African slaves. It took many more years before a civil war ensued and ultimately ended with the abolishment of slavery in 1863-65. (Logan 2009)

Almost four hundred years later, slavery still flourishes in the United States of America. The only difference now is the "value" of the slave. Historically, slaves were a valuable piece of property and that was the incentive to take care of the slaves. In today's context of slavery, the slave is disposable, meaning that they can easily be replaced. Today, slaves are of very little value unless they are bringing in an immediate profit to the trafficker. Traffickers want to minimize the costs incurred as much as possible while maximizing their profits. This is done by paying low wages, if at all, and lowering housing and working conditions to a below poverty level of existence.

"I kept quiet because I have no place to go," says the African woman. Her lips tremble and her voice cracks as she recalls her enslavement--not in Kenya, the country she came from but in America, land of plenty." (Garrett 2008)

Modern day slavery exists in America and most recently showed its presence in North Carolina. This modern day form of slavery is now called human trafficking. According to recent studies, most law enforcement agencies do not believe they have human trafficking crimes occurring in their jurisdictions, but according to the statistics published by the United States Department of Justice in 2009, over 1,229 incidents of human trafficking occurred in the United States between January 1,2007 and September 30, 2008.

A recent report, *Understanding and Improving Law Enforcement Responses to Human Trafficking,* states that upwards to seventy-seven percent (77%) of law enforcement officers think human trafficking is either non-existent or rare in their jurisdiction. As early as 2007, the United States Department of State estimated that 800,000 men, women, and children are trafficked annually throughout the world. It is estimated that about 16,000 of these individuals may find their way to the United States.

In the article, *Imprisoned in the American Nightmare,* author Ronnie Garrett described one woman's unfortunate circumstances.

"Like many before her, she immigrated to the United States filled with promise that she too would be part of the American dream.

'When I arrived into the United States, I was happy,' she recalled. 'I think I'm coming to make friends, to have a good life and to make money.' "But her dreams vanished as she found herself living a nightmare---trapped in a house all day, barred from speaking to anyone, and expected to work grueling hours until she collapsed into bed at night.

'When I'd complain, they'd threaten me ... and I feel so sad ...because when I was in my own country I used to work, I made friends,' she says, and 'Now I come here, I'm locked in the house, not talking to anyone, not going anywhere.'

Luckily this young woman didn't remain hidden in the shadows, though she speaks from them on the DVD I Just Keep Quiet - The Voices of Human Trafficking.' Her ordeal ended when her captors kicked her out of their home. In a strange land, unsure of exactly where she was, she contacted the only person she knew in this country for help. This individual rallied a victim's organization, which was part of a State of Washington Human Trafficking Task Force, to intervene, law enforcement investigated, and as a result of the task force's combined efforts, the criminal wardens received six months house arrest and were ordered to pay restitution."

This is just one case demonstrating the growing crime of modern day slavery and human trafficking. The United States has been recognized as a "country of destination" for those being exported into human trafficking. It is critical we increase our knowledge of human trafficking circumstances and understand our enforcement obligations.

Human Trafficking Statistics

Human trafficking statistics are staggering. Within human trafficking, sex trafficking leads with 82.8% of all suspected cases. Labor trafficking encompasses 11.9% of the human trafficking crimes and another 5.3% are categorized as other or unknown categories. These crimes can and are happening in your hometown.

Law enforcement agencies in small towns are finding trafficking is not just a big-city problem. Cases originate in towns of every size and location. Human trafficking crimes have been documented in towns with populations of less than two thousand, as immigrants are worked in factories and on farms. In addition, there are some misconceptions related to the victims themselves. Any person of vulnerability is susceptible to becoming a victim of human trafficking. This includes children, women, the elderly, etc.

Statistics from an article published by the United States Department of Justice reflect that most suspects in confirmed cases of human trafficking were male (74.3%), Hispanic in origin (38.6%), aged 35 or older (38.2%), and U. S. citizens (56.3%). It is important to reiterate that over half of the human trafficking suspects were legal citizens of our country. (T. Kyckelhahn, A. Beck, and T. Cohen 2009)

In addition, most victims of human trafficking were female (94.4%), of Hispanic origin (61.7%), aged 18-24 years of age (34.1%), and were un-documented aliens (64.4%). Agencies must focus on identifying the victims of human trafficking of any legal status, as well as their traffickers. (Kyckelhahn T., Beck A., and Cohen T. 2009)

With the recent influx of illegal immigrants into our country, these crimes are on the rise and are not being identified appropriately due to them being masked as other crimes, namely those of prostitution, labor camps, exploitation, etc. Recently, several cases of human trafficking with ties to North Carolina received national attention.

North Carolina is a prime target for human trafficking seeing that we are centrally located between New York, NY, and Miami, FL. This location makes our state vulnerable to human trafficking due the accessibility of several major thoroughfares throughout the state, thus providing the traffickers with an effortless means of transporting victims from one destination to another. In addition to our urban areas, North Carolina is known for the rural areas present that employ Hispanic workers, drawing potential human trafficking crimes to our state. We also have many flourishing tourism areas located throughout the state to include destinations from the mountains to the coast. All of these factors make North Carolina a high probability state for being a "destination" for human trafficking.

The United Nations International Labor Organization estimates there are 12.7 million people enslaved worldwide at any given time. Other private organizations estimate the number to be closer to 27 million. The United States Department of State estimates trafficking to be a $32 billion-dollar a year business. (Fisher 2009) Human trafficking is a big business.

To date, human trafficking statistics are difficult to track and are not easily researched since many cases have been intertwined with other related type crimes such as prostitution, pornography, labor law violations, visa violations, etc. One must remember that human trafficking crimes are not researched thoroughly because they are easily masked as other illegal activities within massage parlors, nail shops, and brothels, etc.

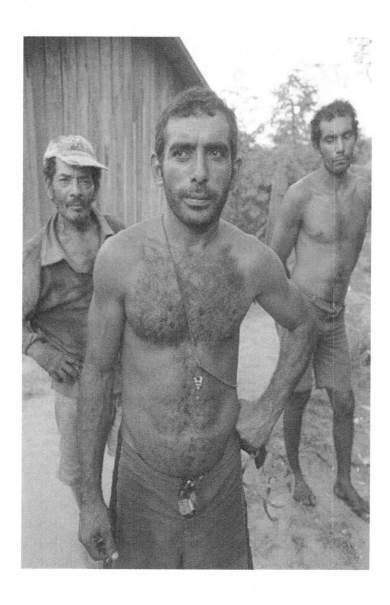

Human Trafficking in North Carolina

Local law enforcement personnel are in the best position to identify human trafficking victims although most local agencies need additional training and instruction to prepare them to handle human trafficking crimes. A recent case in North Carolina involved a Mexican man by the name of Jorge Flores-Rojas being sent to prison for sex trafficking charges as reported in *The News and Observer* newspaper.

In April of 2009, a forty-four year old undocumented Mexican national, by the name of Jorge Flores-Rojas, was sentenced in federal Court in Charlotte, North Carolina to twenty-four years in Federal prison on two counts of sex trafficking of a minor, and one count of interstate transportation of an adult for purposes of a commercial sex act. Flores-Rojas was accused of trafficking a sixteen-year old girl, a seventeen-year old girl, and an adult woman between Washington, DC and Charlotte, NC to perform commercial sex acts in November of 2007. Flores-Rojas pleaded guilty in October of 2008, and was fined $117,000 in restitution to be paid to one of the victims. He was also required to register as a sex offender. He will be deported to Mexico upon his release from prison. The Flores case is one of the first documentations of a human trafficking conviction in North Carolina. The time is now to prepare law enforcement officers to take control and eliminate the human trafficking industry. This is a crime that is only going to worsen before it is eliminated or lessened. (Press 2009)

The time is now to educate our officers on how to identify possible victims of human trafficking. There are many vulnerable populations that are affected by human trafficking. Victims of domestic violence, sexual abuse, and other related crimes are becoming more easily identifiable, but the crimes of human trafficking and the maltreatment including forcing victims to performing labor acts or sexual acts are more difficult to discern. Women and children of poverty stricken homes are also more susceptible to becoming victims of human trafficking.

People that fall to victimization of human trafficking typically are born into slavery, kidnapped, sold, physically forced, or tricked. Being born into slavery is a common form of debt bondage and can last for generations, if not stopped. In other situations, children and adults are kidnapped or physically forced into slavery against their will. In some countries, children are sold into slavery by their parents or guardians. Often times, parents are tricked into giving their children up so their child can supposedly live a better life with more opportunities and/or gain an education. Often this is done for the betterment of the family, but, sadly it is also done for monetary reasons.

So what types of trafficking do we have in the United States? How about in North Carolina? Although studies vary, the majority of the studies show that the sex trade, including prostitution, exotic dancing, pornography, and sex tourism related activities, are the leading types of trafficking occurring in our country. In the "Land of the Free" traffickers employ a large percentage of domestic laborers through agricultural, construction, coal mining, sweatshops, and other begging or trinket selling-type jobs for the purposes of making a profit.

In addition, the food industry employs many victims of trafficking in restaurants and other food services. (Logan 2009) So the question is - do you have any of these establishments in your community? Human trafficking is not unique to rural areas. It is not unique to urban areas. Human trafficking can and is appearing everywhere.

North Carolina has a variety of amenities to offer human traffickers including several major thoroughfares traveling through our state. Interstate 95 and Interstate 40 run directly through North Carolina connecting major east coast cities. These highways provide traffickers with ideal circumstances with which to transport their prisoners. More and more is being documented on human trafficking throughout the United States, although to date, widespread national statistics are not readily available indicating which states are most targeted by traffickers. In addition it is difficult to determine the number of active law enforcement investigations pertaining to human trafficking. All jurisdictions need to raise their level of awareness and be prepared to investigate crimes related to human trafficking.

Chapter 2

What is Human Trafficking?

"Samirah and Enung were recruited from their home in Indonesia by a wealthy family to work in America. Both women signed a contract stating they would be paid U. S. currency in the amount of $100-$200 a month to work in a home taking care of a family. But, when they arrived their passports and travel documents were confiscated and they were made to work close to twenty-one hours a day, to sleep on small mats in the kitchen of the large home, and were given very little to eat. They were threatened, physically assaulted, and rarely allowed out of the house. They were also subjected to what can only be called torture for such transgressions as stealing food because they were often hungry. For example, throughout their time with the family they were forced to run up and down stairs until exhausted, beaten with broom handles and rolling pins, cut with knives, and forced to stand while being scalded with boiling hot water. And for all this, they were not directly paid although some money was sent back to their families in their home country." Both women were close to fifty-years old despite the fact that they spoke very little English which is consistent with victims of human trafficking. (Logan 2009)

This was a prime example of someone coming to our country for a valid reason, so they thought, and being ultimately tricked into enslavement. Although current legislature does not require that someone must be physically transported to meet the elements of human trafficking, many times relocation is used as a method for not being detected and further isolating the victim. The distinct differences of human smuggling and human trafficking will be discussed later in this document.

Defining Human Trafficking

The first problem in combating human trafficking crime is actually defining it; and then getting that information to the officers that are charged with the responsibility of identifying the crime in the field. Many times human trafficking goes undetected due to unfamiliarity with the topic.

The Human Trafficking Victims Protection Act of 2000 (TVPA) defines labor trafficking as, "the recruitment, harboring, transportation, provision, or obtaining of a person for labor or services, through the use of force, fraud, or coercion for the purpose of subjection to involuntary servitude, peonage, debt bondage, or slavery." The TVPA reauthorizations 2003, 2005, and 2008 included, "person was induced to perform labor or a commercial sex act through force, fraud or coercion. Any person under the age of eighteen who performs a commercial sex act is considered a victim of human trafficking, regardless of whether force, fraud or coercion was present." (Trafficking Victims Protection Act 2000) This definition will most certainly be expanded as recognition of human trafficking crimes is more widely exposed.

Let's discuss some of terms listed in the TVPA such as the requirement of force, fraud, or coercion. These factors are required to meet the elements of the TVPA if the victim is at least eighteen years old. Remember that the TVPA does not require force, fraud, or coercion if the victim is a person under the age of eighteen who performs a commercial sex act.

Force refers to the use of sexual assault, physical assaults, and/or confinement to maintain control over another person. (United States Department of Health and Human Services, Human Trafficking Fact Sheet 2009)

Fraud often times refers to false promises made to the victim that induces someone to enter a highly probable trafficking situation. An example could be someone agreeing to be smuggled into a country but then upon arrival the smuggler increases the cost of the transportation enough where the person cannot uphold their agreement and now they must work for the trafficker in attempt to repay their debt. Often, the victim does not know that this is not an enforceable agreement in the United States and feels that it is their obligation to repay the money. This voluntary smuggling transaction has just changed into a trafficking crime due to the fraudulent terms related in the agreement and the inability for the victim to pay the debt owed. (United States Department of Health and Human Services, Human Trafficking Fact Sheet 2009)

Coercion refers to the use of threats, or physical restraint against any person. It could also refer to a plan intended to cause a person to believe that failure to uphold their end of the agreement, serious harm will occur against them, their family, or friend. Often, abuse or threatened abuse of the legal process is also used as a control method. (Human Trafficking Fact Sheet 2009)

Differences between Human Trafficking and Human Smuggling

If the general public is asked to define the difference between human trafficking and human smuggling, many say that the terms are used interchangeably. This is not a true statement. Human trafficking and human smuggling are two very different crimes although the act of human smuggling could at some point become an act of human trafficking. If the victims are dependent upon the trafficker for basic life function, this may be an indicator of trafficking.

The United States Immigration and Customs Enforcement (ICE) define smuggling as, "the importation of people into the U. S. involving deliberate evasion of immigration laws. This offense includes bringing illegal aliens into the U. S., as well as, the unlawful transportation and harboring of aliens already in the U. S." Smuggling is transportation-based and trafficking is exploitation-based. Trafficking does not require transportation or border crossing and does not only happen to immigrants or foreign nationals.

Summarily, smuggling is a crime against the country's sovereignty, whereas trafficking is a crime against another person. The main difference between human trafficking and human smuggling is whether the individual has the ability to make their own decisions rather than being forced into a situation of exploitation where there freedom has been stripped from them. Granted, when someone makes a decision to be smuggled into a country this can very quickly turn into a human trafficking case when the trafficker does not follow through with the initial smuggling plan. Many trafficking cases stem from individuals being smuggled into a country and then held against their will through coercion, force, or fraud. (Women n.d.)

Furthermore, smuggling often times will instigate a crime of human trafficking. The cases goes something like this...first a smuggler and an illegal immigrant make an agreement to bring the illegal immigrant into the country for a certain amount of money or other form of compensation. Upon arrival at their destination site the trafficker does not comply with their initial agreement forcing the illegal immigrant to rely on the smuggler/trafficker to meet their everyday needs until the debt owed can be paid off. The person being smuggled is now a victim of human trafficking since they are now being coerced or forced into an agreement that they did not initially agree upon. Their vulnerability and desire to enter the country makes them an easy target for traffickers. Traffickers then feed on their want and desire to remain in the country fraudulently forcing them to perform acts involuntarily.

Types of Human Trafficking

Human trafficking can be divided into several categories that include labor trafficking and sex trafficking.

Labor Trafficking

According to the United States Department of Health and Human Services, labor trafficking can be further categorized as:

> **1. Bonded labor or debt bondage** - least known but most widely used method to enslave people; repayment for loan or service. The value of their work is greater than the original sum of money "borrowed." This occurs when the victim's labor is required for repayment of a loan or service whereas the terms and/or conditions were not clearly defined. The value of the victim's services/labor is assessed and is not

applied towards the debt owed to the perpetrator.

2. Forced labor - victim is forced to work against their own will, by threats of violence or some other form of punishment. The victim's freedom is restricted. Some examples include domestic servitude, agricultural labor, sweatshop factory labor, janitorial, food service and other service industry labor, and begging.

Child victims of human trafficking are exceedingly vulnerable and typically easy to maintain control over. There are several hazards associated with child labor that affect them physically, mentally, spiritually, morally, and socially. The International Labor Organization estimates that there are 246,000,000 children between the ages of five and seventeen involved in child labor crimes. Examples include forced recruitment for armed conflict, child prostitution, child pornography, illegal drug trade, and illegal arms trade. (Labor Trafficking Fact Sheet 2009)

Labor trafficking may involve young children, teenagers, men, or women. These victims are found in factory environments, construction sites, drug and arms trade, and simple street panhandling schemes. Officers should be ever vigilant in all environments. The United States Department of State says that more than half of all human trafficking victims are children. (Child Victims of Human Trafficking 2009)

Sex Trafficking

A second type of trafficking involves the sex trade. This occurs when a commercial sex act is committed by force, fraud, or coercion or the person is under the age of 18. According to the TVPA the term "commercial sex act" refers to a sex act when anything of value is given or received by any person. Many times victims may get a job as an exotic dancer or as a stripper in various clubs or brothels and then they are placed in a position of coercion by forcing them to participate in acts of commercial sex such as pornography and prostitution.

According to the United States Department of Health and Human Services Sex Trafficking Fact Sheet, there are various types of sex-trafficking crimes that are related to human trafficking. These crimes may include:

- Prostitution
- Pornography
- Stripping
- Live-sex shows
- Mail-order brides
- Military prostitution
- Sex tourism

Potential victims of sex trafficking include women, men, girls, and boys, although the majority are women and girls.

Traffickers lure potential victims into sex trafficking with a promise of a good job in another country or location within the country, a false marriage proposal turning into a bondage situation, selling the individual into the sex trade (sometimes by parents, husbands, or boyfriends), and kidnapping scenarios. (Sex Trafficking Fact Sheet n.d.)

Traffickers employ various methods to "condition" their victims. They may use starvation, confinement, physical abuse, rape, gang rape, threats of violence toward the victim and their families, forced drug use, or a threat of shaming the victim to their friends and family. (Sex Trafficking Fact Sheet 2009)

Traffickers frequently use debt-bondage as a method to maintain control over the victim telling the victim they must "work off" their debts to the perpetrator. Many times, this financial obligation is also a moral obligation that the victims feels is necessary to satisfy whatever debt has been incurred in honor of their family name.

In addition, the trafficker isolates the victim from their family and friends and even from their ethnic or religious community. They confiscate passports, visas, and other forms of identification documents. They use threats of violence toward the victim and/or the victim's family or friends. They often will tell the victim that they are committing a crime and if they report it to local law enforcement, "they will be punished" or arrested and deported. Perpetrators usually control the finances of the victim leaving the victim with little or no financial resources. This form of control establishes a co-dependency situation where the victim is dependent upon the perpetrator for their everyday needs of living.

Sex trafficking victims may also suffer from traumatic bonding. Traumatic bonding refers to a form of coercive control where the victim fears the perpetrator; as well as the victim develops a feeling of gratitude towards the trafficker, for being allowed to live.

Sex trafficking can occur in underground systems or public systems, closed brothels - not open to new customers (can't do a sting and send someone in undercover if they don't accept new clients), residential homes, massage parlors, spas, strip clubs, and other businesses used as fronts for prostitution. (Sex Trafficking Fact Sheet 2009)

There are two major known sex trafficking networks operating in the United States:

> 1.   Asian sex trafficking networks such as commercial-front Asian massage parlors, Asian room salons/hostess clubs or karaoke bars, Asian residential brothels, and Asian escort services.

> 2.   Latino sex trafficking networks such as Latino residential brothels, Latino cantina bars, and Latino escort/ "delivery" services.

> 3.   Other sex trafficking networks may include international marriage brokers/servile marriage, mail order brides, and personal sexual servitude.

How to Identify a Human Trafficking Crime

Updated community policing programs can play an important role in identifying trafficking situations.   This positive relationship with community members can lead to information that uncovers trafficking situations. Victims can fail to recognize their plight or not otherwise understand the seriousness of their lifestyle. One goal of law enforcement is to provide potential victims with enough information to allow them to avoid the situation or at the very least identify their own situation as trafficking, whether sex or labor-related.

Most victims do not identify themselves as victims of human trafficking. Officer compassion is crucial to gaining trust and information in these cases and critical information may be forthcoming after several attempts have been made to interview the victim. Persistence and patience is critical in these types of investigations.

How to Identify a Victim of Human Trafficking

There is no specific face to a human trafficking victim. Trafficked persons can be rich or poor, men or women, adults or children, and foreign nationals or U. S. citizens. The next victim of human trafficking could be your wife, husband, mother, father, daughter, son, sister, brother, niece or nephew. This crime shows no prejudice in choosing its next victim.

However, there are some indicators of an adult human trafficking victim which include the following:

- They may have few or no personal possessions and few or no personal financial records.

- They may be asked about their whereabouts and do not know what city they are in

- "Branded" with their trafficker's name

- Work excessively long and unusual hours and may not be allowed breaks at work.

- They may live in locations with security measures such as barbed wire, guarded compounds, bars on the outside of windows, or boarded up windows.

- There may be numerous inconsistencies in their story

- Be afraid of law enforcement officers

- Avoid eye contact

- Exhibit paranoid behavior.

- Loss their sense of time or space.

Children involved in human trafficking are most often under the age of 18. Some countries, which have shown to be sources of child victims, include the Pacific Islands, the former Soviet Union, Latin America, Southeast Asia and Africa, as well as other third world developing countries.

"Half the victims of human trafficking may be children under 18," according to John Miller, Director of the United States Department of State, Office to Monitor and Combat Trafficking in Persons. The current rate of children being trafficked is already ten times higher than the transatlantic slave trade at its peak. It is the fastest growing form of forced labor in our country's history. (Make Way Partners n.d.)

Be aware that children can also be trafficked by close family members. The child may think they are being united with family in the United States, or recruited to work a legitimate job. They may be under the impression that they are being brought to the United States in order to attend better schools. All is not what it may seem.

According to the United States Department of Health and Human Services, indicators of a child victim of human trafficking may include the following:

- Child may be hungry/malnourished

- Child may never reach full height

- Child may have rotten or ill taken care of teeth

- Child may have reproductive problems

- Child lives at the workplace

- Child may be living with multiple people in a cramped space

- Child may be attending school sporadically or not at all

How to Prosecute a Human Trafficking Case

Although prosecution is discussed subsequently in Chapter 6 it is important to make note that a human trafficking prosecution can take months, if not years. Therefore, it is of the essence that your agency keeps track of the victim and/or victims. Non-governmental organizations and social service providers can assist law enforcement agencies with this duty. Keep in mind that many human trafficking victims turn to drug or commercial sex because they feel they have no other desirable attributes to offer in their lives.

During the investigation of human trafficking cases, law enforcement officers should seize any monies involved. During restitution these funds can be transferred to the victim to compensate them for trauma.

We will discuss federal and state laws applicable in Chapter 6. It is important for you to understand the definitions and statutes related to the crime of human trafficking. Please refer to your Attorney General's Office for further resources in your state. Included are related North Carolina general statutes.

Chapter 3

Law Enforcement Protocols

"An anti-trafficking hotline received a call from a man who said he has been to a brothel, where he met a Central American woman who cried and said she was afraid the brothel operators would hurt her family in her home country if she did not prostitute. The caller said the brothel is next to a migrant labor community and the women in the brothel were undocumented and afraid of being deported." (Moossy n.d.)

Developing Human Trafficking Courses for Law Enforcement Officers

In 2008, The North Carolina Justice Academy developed a Human Trafficking Protocols course in efforts to educate officers across the state about human trafficking. The course is available for any law enforcement officer wishing to obtain information on human trafficking and understanding the dynamics of the crime. The course is designed to enhance the officer's ability to identify forms of exploitation associated with human trafficking, as well as, to discuss strategies in investigating crimes related to human trafficking. Officers are provided the tools to recognize the many indicators of human trafficking. During the course, officers are provided with a list of agencies that aid in investigating crimes of this nature, such as the Federal Bureau of Investigation (FBI), the United States

Attorney's Office, the United States Immigration and Customs Enforcement (ICE) and others. In 2009, the North Carolina Justice Academy created yet another educational tool, a four-hour web-based human trafficking course for law enforcement personnel in efforts to enhance the awareness level of law enforcement.

Joining Efforts with Other Organizations

Law enforcement agencies can join with other organizations to battle human trafficking crimes. North Carolina has become a leader in forming a statewide organization for this purpose.

In 2004, an organization was formed in North Carolina to determine the extent of human trafficking incidents in the state. On April 22, 2004, RIPPLE (**R**ecognition, **I**dentification, **P**rotection, **P**rosecution, **L**iberation, **E**mpowerment) was established. RIPPLE was formed by a group of concerned parties including the North Carolina Attorney General's Office/Victim and Citizens Services Section and the North Carolina Coalition Against Sexual Assault. Approximately thirty-five individuals from various local, state, and federal agencies attended. Presently, RIPPLE is comprised of over seventy members from organizations such as the Bureau of Immigration and Customs Enforcement (ICE), United States Attorney's Office, Federal Bureau of Investigation (FBI), North Carolina Department of Labor, North Carolina State Highway Patrol, North Carolina Department of Justice, North Carolina Coalition Against Domestic Violence, North Carolina Coalition Against Sexual Assault, Legal Aid of North Carolina, World Relief, and the North Carolina Justice Academy.

The North Carolina Justice Academy is working diligently with RIPPLE to assist officers in recognizing and identifying crimes of human trafficking, while working together with other agencies to protect victims and prosecute suspects of human trafficking.

Other areas of the country, such as Northwestern University, are examining the factors connected with human trafficking and becoming partners with various prevention organizations. As early as 2006, federal grants were awarded by the United States Department of Justice funding collaborative efforts to fight human trafficking. The Human Trafficking Rescue Project in western Missouri was just one of several organizations who are laying the groundwork for establishing laws and procedures against human trafficking. Other towns like Seattle and Washington, dubbed the Asian gateway, are targeting human trafficking and developing programs against human trafficking. Attention has been centered on educating the public and officers about this crime.

It is important to recognize that human trafficking is difficult to identify and that one must begin by educating the law enforcement community to recognize the "red flags" or possible indicators of human trafficking.

Overcoming the prejudice towards the victim is another crucial key to the success of combating human trafficking. With the influx of illegal immigrants into our country, the prejudice towards them is at a peak. Given that the majority of human trafficking victims are undocumented, this is a bias that must be overcome in order to assist them adequately. Keep in mind that the majority of all human trafficking victims and suspects are of Hispanic origin. Typically, victims of human trafficking are undocumented aliens while human traffickers are documented citizens.

Human trafficking is a global issue being addressed. Worldwide, the media could assist in raising the awareness level about human trafficking by providing objective information to the general public and possible victims of human trafficking. These proactive approaches could provide resources available to someone that finds him or herself in a situation that they do not want to be in or it could further protect someone from being victimized in the future.

Building Partnerships with Other Organizations

It is imperative that we build partnerships with all organizations that come into contact with vulnerable populations to ensure the identification of possible human trafficking victims. Human trafficking task forces benefit by having members represented from the local law enforcement agencies, social services department, health department, emergency medical system, hospitals, shelters, etc. All of these entities come into contact with highly probable victims of human trafficking on a daily basis. Being prepared before an act of human trafficking occurs is the key to a proactive approach to addressing human trafficking and the needs of their victims.

Most victims of human trafficking do not initially identify themselves as a victim so it is important that we take on the responsibility to identify them by recognizing the "red flags" present before a crime occurs. These "red flags" are only indicators and they are not a confirmation that someone is a victim, although it is a good place to initiate an investigation. With all criminal behaviors, law enforcement officers must be able to articulate the circumstances of the case in order to establish probable cause. Many times law enforcement can only be reactive to a crime, although, this is a crime that we can be proactive in efforts to be prepared in the event that an incident occurs and to possibly eliminate the problem before it ensues.

Meeting the Needs of Victims

Like any victims of abuse, victims of human trafficking have unique needs that are specific to the crime. These needs may be physical, psychological, or emotional depending on the victim's ability to cope with the victimization. Victims of human trafficking often walk away from a situation with only the clothes on their back. They may or may not have identity documentation, passports, or any form of identification. They may not even speak the language. They have no way to support their self, no place to live, and no transportation. Culturally, they may not understand what is happening to them or why. These victims have suffered short- and long-term abuse both emotionally and physically, which require special assistance. Victims of human trafficking have a far greater safety concern for themselves and their family members back home. Many will not cooperate with law enforcement in hopes that the trafficker will not hurt them or their family.

Chapter 4

Interviewing the Victims

"Every day silence harvests its victims. Silence is a mortal illness." -Natalia Ginzburg

Investigators conducting interviews in suspected cases of human trafficking must remember that basic everyday domestic violence, child abuse, or neglect cases may be more than meets the eye. The first step in interviewing the potential human trafficking victim is to...

- Establish rapport and reassure the victim that they are safe now.

- Reassure them that you are here to help them and recognize that they are the victim and not a criminal, even if involved in illegal activity.

- Tell them they can apply for special visas and other forms of immigration/ refugee relief and that you will be sure to refer them to the appropriate agencies to assist them with this step.

- Reassure them that what happened to them is "wrong" and they deserve better.

- Tell them that they have the right to live without being abused.

- Reassure them that they can trust the law enforcement. Assure them that you want to work with them so that what happened to them does not happen to others.

- Assure them that they have legal rights to protect them against this type of crime. Victims are entitled to assistance and you are here to help them. (Anderson 2008)

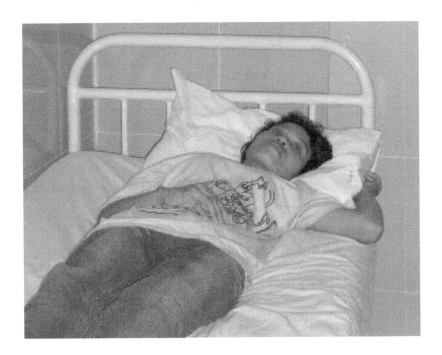

Important Factors to Determine During the Investigation

Many of the same interviewing techniques can help the officer to effectively interview the victim to determine if, in fact, a human trafficking crime has occurred. Some of the factors to consider include:

- Does the victim seem more nervous than usual?

- Is the victim cooperative?

- Does the victim have free access to coming and leaving the residence?

- Are there marks on wrists or legs indicating shackles or chains (indicators of confinement)?

- Does the victim live or sleep in small, cramped quarters?

- If from a foreign country, does the victim have access and can he/she produce immigration papers? Passport? Birth certificate? Driver's license?

- How long has the individual lived in the area (traffickers often move victims frequently)?

- What type of work do they do? What is their pay rate?

- How old is the victim? Can they readily tell you their birth date and year?

- If the victim does not speak English well, are official interpreters available? (Avoid allowing the potential trafficker to act as the interpreter, as well as, other suspected victims. Another victim may actually be a trafficker in disguise or involved in the trafficking process.)

As stated in the North Carolina Justice Academy Human Trafficking Protocols course, there are many questions that need to be asked in a human trafficking investigation. All of these questions aid in establishing the use of force, fraud, or coercion. (Anderson 2008)

Additional interview questions might include:

- Were you ever threatened if you tried to leave?

- Witness any threats against others trying to leave?

- Has your family been threatened?

- Do you know of any other people's family being threatened or ever been threatened?

- Ever physically abused or witness physical abuse towards others?

- What type of physical abuse?

- Objects used? Weapons involved?

- Ever reported before and to whom?

- How are medical problems handled? Attended to by whom?

- How did you get your job?

- How did you get in this country?

- Who brought you here?

- Did you come for a specific job or promise?

- Who promised you a job?

- Were you forced to do different work than initially agreed upon?

- Was there a prepared contract?

- Who made your travel arrangements?

- Who paid for your travel?

- Are you getting paid for your work?

- Do you receive payment or is your money being held for you for so-called "safe-keeping?"

- Do you owe your employer money?

- Where are your financial records/receipts?

- How are you paid? Cash, check, money order, etc.?

- Do you have possession of your legal documents? If no, why?

- Were you provided false documents?

- Are you being made to do something you do not want to do?

- Is your freedom of movement restricted?

- Do you live, sleep, and work in the same place?

- Where does the alleged perpetrator live/eat/sleep?

- Are the conditions the same for both victim and perpetrator?

- What are the conditions when you are left unattended?

- Were physical restraints used such as locks, chains, etc? If so, who has the keys?

- How did you get around town? Car, van, bus, subway, etc.?

- Who supervises your travel around town?

- How do you get medicines/prescriptions, if needed?

- Are you allowed to watch television, listen to radio, or read newspapers, magazines?

- Do you have telephone access or Internet access?

- Who are you afraid of and why?

- What would you like to see happen to the people who hurt you?

- How do you feel about the police?

Investigators should record all verbal and non-verbal behaviors provided by the victim. Behavioral indicators may help to identify physical or psychological symptoms. Verbal responses should be recorded verbatim. The mindset of the human trafficking victim is typically not the norm and may involve many of these indicators.

Establishing Rapport

Victims of human trafficking are often taught or brainwashed to distrust law enforcement and the government. They fear possible deportation and often feel their situation is their own fault. They may or may not have an emotional attachment to their captor. Even though their current condition may be extremely bad, it may possibly be worse where they came from, regardless of the beatings and/or rapes incurred. There are social, ethical and cultural differences present in understanding the victim's demeanor and reactions. It is essential to be able recognize and address this diversity when interviewing victims of human trafficking. Being sensitive to the victim's needs will assist you in establishing rapport. They may have been intentionally misinformed of their rights by the perpetrator and unaware of available assistance. Many victims do not self-identify as victims and do not see themselves as in need of assistance. They fear for their safety and the safety of their family. They would rather stay in the present situation than risk harm to their loved ones.

Investigators must remain objective throughout the investigation and refrain from involving their personal opinion. Interview victims separately, watch to see if one victim looks to the other for confirmation, as some victims are promoted to being enforcers. Do not stop investigating because the victim lies; this may be a survival technique for them as they have been brain washed to be fearful of a law enforcement officer because either the trafficker has threatened them repeatedly with harm or harming their families.

Investigators must understand the importance of building rapport with the victim. The victim may also be in the country illegally and fear deportation. They will need continual reassurance that law enforcement will help them throughout this process of rebuilding their lives.

When questioning the victim, information that you want to acquire includes the following:

- Working conditions

- Living conditions

- Indications of restriction of movement

- Whether they are forced to make frequent moves

- Behavioral indicators of dependency such as submissiveness or fearfulness in the presence of another

- Determine who is in physical possession of legal documents/identification documents including their citizenship status

Evidence Collection

Collect any evidence identifying other related crimes associated with human trafficking such as the following:

- Prostitution

- Operations of massage parlors, strip clubs, etc.

- Domestic abuse

- "False" 911 calls

- Vice raids where foreign nationals are found

- Encounters with migrant workers, such as on farms or construction sites (separate from supervisor interviews)

- Fights between people over money

- Crimes involving immigrant children such as child prostitution or forced labor

Investigators should be looking for evidence that corroborates the victim's statement such as testimony of other victims and witnesses, or physical evidence. One victim can lead you to several other victims. Remember that the investigators must establish that coercion, fraud or force was used in the commission of the act unless it involved a minor.

Physical evidence to collect may include documents such as brothel ledgers (sometimes written in crypt or code) photographs of the victims being transported, tally sheets, telephone numbers, bank records, victim diaries, provocative clothing, condoms, lubricants, sex paraphernalia, and digital evidence located in cell phones, text messages, iPods, and laptops.

Investigators must be patient - obtaining truthful statements often takes several interviews, over weeks or months, as the victim begins the healing process. This stems from the history of the victim being told to distrust law enforcement. Demonstrating respect, compassion, and understanding for the emotional and physical trauma related to the human trafficking crime will aid you in gaining truthful statements from the victims.

Investigators should use covert methods to gather evidence first before considering other methods such as a raid. Covert operations with cameras; consensually monitored telephone calls, tracking devices, and undercover operatives are all suggested measures to gain intelligence.

Investigators should photograph and video the interior and exterior of the building during the execution of the search warrant. Try to capture the living conditions and signage outside, any photographs lying around, locks and other restraints present, or any posted rules or notices. All of this evidence can help corroborate the victim's statements.

In addition, investigators can interview nearby clothing store clerks that sell provocative clothing for customer's behavior and freedom of movement, even though they did not observe a crime occur. Clothing store clerks could testify to the control one person appeared to have over another as observed during the shopping interaction.

In a documented situation, "A police officer at a mall was approached by a frantic and scared young woman running from a store that sells provocative women's clothing. She asked for help and said she was being held against her will. Later, she told police that she was a U. S. citizen and was being beaten by a pimp who was forcing her to prostitute herself in motels throughout the area." An approachable mall officer was able to investigate and assist this young woman. (Moossy n.d.) You just never know where the next call about human trafficking is going to come from…

Chapter 5

Treatment Plans for the Victim

"You gain strength, courage and confidence by every experience in which you really stop to look fear in the face. You are able to say to yourself, "I lived through this horror. I can take the next thing that comes along."

-Eleanor Roosevelt, 1960

Victims see safety as the most critical need after exposing the crime of human trafficking. It is a personal choice to cooperate in interviews and prosecution of the perpetrators. Rapport must be developed and a plan put into action to address the needs of the victim.

Esperanza, a trafficking victim survivor stated, "When I started cooperating with law enforcement, everything they promised me was true. I felt comfortable; I believe in them; I trust them. So I decided to go, to cooperate, to speak out, and to help others who are not able to speak out because of fear." (Police 2006) The necessity of building that victim rapport cannot be overemphasized.

Treatment plans should include a multi-agency approach. Various organizations can fill roles to provide assistance to the victim such as addressing their physical

51

safety, seeking treatment for sexual trauma, treatment of illnesses, nourishment, clothing, medications, mental health services, childcare, or other immediate needs. These basic needs must be met to be successful to assist the victim in the recovery process.

There are many reasons why victims of human trafficking stay in their present situation. Four reasons come to mind when victims are asked why they stay in abusive relationships. The first is fear....fear which keeps people from leaving a dangerous situation. The fear may be for their own personal safety or that of a loved one.

Secondly, the victim may have a lack of knowledge about individual and personal rights, which keeps them from leaving their abuser or trafficker. Imagine that you are a captive in a foreign country where you do not speak the language nor do you have the knowledge to be able to contact law enforcement. You may even think that the police in that country are corrupt. Where would you turn? Who would you turn to?

Thirdly, similar to domestic violence relationships and abuse, many power and control tactics can and are employed to gain control over another person. Such tactics include utilizing isolation from the victim's family, friends, or other social networking organizations, intimidation, emotional abuse, economic abuse, and the use of coercion and threats. Confinement can also be used, both physically and psychologically. There does not need to be a lock on the door to confine someone psychologically. In addition, the victim may have never been physically assaulted although they fear that they will be harmed if they were to leave. Fear is a powerful tool used to control another person.

Lastly, the mere thought of someone hurting your family might convince you to stay in a bad situation even if you are not being physically assaulted or abused. These controlling behaviors may be visible or they may be hidden. Again, it is vital to separate the victim from other victims as well as from the suspected trafficker(s). Traffickers will employ other "so-called" female victims to supervise their victims even though they are in essence a trafficker as well. Who appears to be a victim on the outside may not necessarily be a victim, indeed they may be a trafficker. In many cases, there's more than meets the eye. Recognizing what indicators are present will aid you in your identification and investigation process.

Understanding the Victim's Trauma

Victims of human trafficking endure both physical and psychological abuse sometimes over many years of rape and/or torture. Officers cannot hope to understand the experience but must recognize the emotional and physical devastation, which may be connected with any human trafficking occurrence. Compassion and patience will help the victim learn to trust law enforcement. Barriers of distrust or fear are not uncommon for these victims. Law enforcement officers must recognize and be prepared to deal with these human emotions and experiences. Treatment may involve physical health, mental health, housing, education, employment, and many other agencies that can collaborate to provide the needed services. Local agencies are also encouraged to involve federal agencies, which may have additional resources available.

Language Barriers

In addition, language barriers compound the trauma of confronting a human trafficking crime. Often, victims of human trafficking do not speak English, therefore, making it difficult to gather the information needed for your investigation. Requesting a certified translator is crucial to obtaining truthful statements from the victim(s). Allowing a family member, friend, or another victim translate may hinder your investigation by providing false or misinformed information. Although the translator may have good intentions, they may alter your victim's statements in a way that is damaging to your investigation. In some cases, what appeared to be another victim actually turned out to be a trafficker.

Treatment Plans

In the course of processing a human trafficking case, the victim should be provided with appropriate referrals to address all of the potential human services needs that may occur. Each agency should pre-plan but also design a custom treatment plan and protocol for each human trafficking victim. Specific needs may be addressed in a comprehensive treatment plan. This plan may include the following:

> **Physical Safety Issues** - creating a plan for the immediate, short-term and long-term protection of the victim and their family

Physical Needs - nourishment (food and any additional special needs that might be required such as diabetic medicines, etc.)

Shelter - short-term and long-term housing

Clothing - does the victim have or need clothing? Most victims walk away from a situation with only the clothes on their back.

Pets - can any pets be provided for or allowed to remain with the victim? This may be the only trusted connection for emotional support for the victim.

Sexual Trauma Treatments - includes the following:

- Physical needs – treatment and/or prescriptions

- Psychological needs - possible mental health treatment

Physical Health Plans - Physical health examination and treatment, as well as, needed medications or other health needs.

Mental Health Services –includes the following:

- Mental health evaluation

- Post traumatic stress disorder (PTSD) and other disorders being diagnosed and treated

- Substance abuse assessment

Child Care Services - as needed to allow the victim the ability to pursue employment, services, and obtain other living necessities.

Follow-up Schedule and Case Management - Create a follow-up schedule and assign a case manager for each case. This may be an individual outside of the law enforcement agency such as a social services case manager.

Other immediate needs - to include both short-term and long-term resources as the case may demand.

Health Risks of Human Trafficking

There are many health risks for the victims of human trafficking. Some may be obvious and some latent or not as visible upon first inspection. Among those are:

- Sleeping and eating disorders

- Sexually transmitted diseases such as HIV/AIDS; pelvic pain; rectal trauma; urinary tract infections, from working the sex industry; vaginal/anal tears; gonorrhea; syphilis; pubic lice; sterility; miscarriages; menstrual problems; and forced or coerced abortions

- Chronic back pain

- Hearing loss

- Cardiovascular or respiratory problems from endless days in agricultural jobs, sweatshop environments, or construction conditions

- Physical abuse, scars, broken bones, concussions, and burns

- Headaches, traumatic brain injury, memory loss, dizziness, or numbness

- Limb amputation

- Substance abuse

- Communicable diseases such as Tuberculosis, Hepatitis, Malaria, and Pneumonia

- Other physical ailments

A complete physical examination by a certified physician is warranted in all cases of child human trafficking, and advised in cases of adult trafficking (with the consent of the individual). In cases of child trafficking, the Department of Human Services (Social Services) can assist in determining the appropriateness of a complete health examination, particularly after a law enforcement intervention, interviews, and referral to appropriate agencies. Adult victims should be encouraged to seek appropriate health examinations and given appropriate referrals for available services as well.

According to the United States Department of Health and Human Services Labor Trafficking Fact Sheet, one should expect that psychological problems may be present and potential risks might include:

- Excessive fear and acute anxiety

- Sense of helplessness

- Depression and mood changes, denial, and/or disbelief

- Guilt, humiliation, grief, fear, distrust, self-hatred, and shame

- Cultural shock from finding themselves in a strange environment/country

- Post traumatic stress disorder (PTSD)

- Shock – a sense of numbness or lack of feelings

- Disorientation and confusion, mind/body separation/disassociation of ego status

- Phobias, panic attacks, insomnia, physical hyper-alertness, self loathing, and/or resistance to change

- Hatred of men (or women), suicidal attempts or ideations; specialized assistance may be needed for victims of torture

- Other mental disorders including traumatic bonding with the perpetrator of the crime such as the *Stockholm syndrome*. In these situations there are cognitive distortions where the victim reciprocates positive feelings towards the perpetrator and the other victims. This is a type of mental survival skill/coping mechanism.

All victims of human trafficking should be encouraged to seek out a complete mental health evaluation and given appropriate service contacts. Full treatment plans should also include referral to agencies that may provide guidance to assist the victim in:

- Obtaining a valid visa or other identification papers

- Placement in appropriate housing such as foster or group homes

- Obtaining independent living arrangements appropriate to the victim's developmental, physical, and mental needs

- Obtaining intensive case management through appropriate agency referrals

- Enrollment into educational institutions, job training programs, appropriate employment opportunities, and English courses (if needed)

- Obtaining transportation for a family reunification, or other services needed to integrate them back into mainstream society

Special assistance is available for sex trafficking victims. The United States Department of Health and Human Services can help the victim with their immigration status. By certifying victims of trafficking, the United States Department of Health and Human Services enables trafficking victims who are non-U. S. citizens to receive federally funded benefits and services similar to those benefits that refugees receive. To become certified the victim must cooperate with the investigation and prosecution of the perpetrator. Victims of trafficking who are U. S. citizens do not need to be certified to receive benefits and may already be eligible for many benefits. Services include but are not limited to, food, health care, and employment assistance.

Federal Assistance

The following agencies can be contacted for assistance in human trafficking cases:

Federal Bureau of Investigation (FBI) – investigates and prosecutes cases of human trafficking. They also coordinate victim services throughout the investigation and/or prosecution. According to an article published by the Government Accountability Office, the FBI has investigated 751 trafficking cases between 2001 and April 5, 2007. The numbers of cases opened has increased: from 15 in 2001 to 70 in 2006. These investigations include joint efforts with U. S. Immigrations and Customs Enforcement (ICE). (Human trafficking: A strategic framework could help enhance the interagency collaboration needed to effectively combat trafficking crimes 2007).

Trafficking Victims Protection Act of 2000 (TVPA) – was originally enacted in October of 2000. Its mission is to prevent human trafficking overseas, protect victims, help them rebuild their lives in the United States with federal and state support, and to prosecute traffickers of persons under stiff federal penalties. In 2003, the act was reauthorized and applied more than $200,000,000 to combat human trafficking. It also encourages the nation's 21,000 state and local law enforcement agencies to participate in the detection and investigation of human trafficking.

Presently, the United States Department of Justice has funded forty-two jurisdictions and thirty-six trafficking victim services providers to form human trafficking task forces to identify and rescue victims by proactively investigating such cases. These task forces include federal, state and local law enforcement agencies and victim services organizations to investigate all forms of human trafficking and assist the victims during the investigation and prosecution process. The task forces also provide training on identifying human trafficking cases and potential victims. North Carolina has a Human Trafficking Task Force located in Pitt County, North Carolina. The North Carolina Justice Academy (NCJA) is working diligently with them to aid in the education of law enforcement officers across the state.

United States Department of Health and Human Services - certifies victims of human trafficking once they have been identified by law enforcement. This certification allows the victim to receive federally funded benefits and services to the same extent as refugees. According to the United States Department of State Trafficking in Persons Report: 2007, 1,379 foreign national victims of human trafficking were certified through by the Department of Health and Human Services from October 2000 through fiscal year 2007. Of the persons certified, 131 were minors and 1,248 were adults originating from seventy-seven different countries.

To receive certification, victims of trafficking must be a victim of a severe form of trafficking as defined by TVPA Act of 2000, and be willing to assist with the investigation and prosecution process, and have completed a bona fide application for a T visa, or received a continued presence status from United States Department of Homeland Security. Please note that children of human trafficking DO NOT need to be certified to receive services or benefits.

United States Department of Health and Human Services-Rescue and Restore Campaign Information and Referral Hotline 1-888-3737-888

T Visa: allow victims of severe trafficking to become temporary residents of the U. S. Many times it may not be in the victim's best interest to return to their country of origin and that victims need this time to rebuild their lives.

After three years of having a T visa, they may be eligible for permanent residence if he/she meets the following conditions:

- They are a person of good moral character.

- They have complied with any reasonable request for assistance in the investigation during the past three years.

- They will suffer extreme hardship if they are removed from this country (many times it is not in the victim's best interest to return to their country of origin).

63

According to the United States Department of State, Trafficking in Persons Report: 2007, there were over one thousand T visas granted by the Department of Homeland Security from October 1, 2000 through November 31, 2008 to human trafficking survivors. In addition there were over one thousand derivative T visas granted to family members. Presently, the Department of Homeland Security is authorized to issue up to five thousand T-visas per year.

United States Department of Homeland Security - U. S. Immigration and Customs Enforcement (ICE), investigates cases of human trafficking, adjudicates and continues presence status, which makes the victim eligible for certification. ICE reported that they had 899 open cases from 2005 to May 31, 2007 with 557 of them being sexual exploitation, 257 of them being forced labor, and 85 of them as other. ICE reported that they received 264 convictions. Of the convictions, 129 of them were sexual exploitation, 17 were forced labor, and 118 of them were classified as other. ICE works with law enforcement and other worldwide networks to identify, rescue, and provide assistance to trafficking victims utilizing a victim-centered approach. For more information or to contact ICE: www.ice.gov or call 1-866-DHS-2-ICE or 1-866-347-2423

United States Department of Justice - investigates and prosecutes cases of human trafficking; have contributed to the construction of a network on trafficking victim's service providers via grants, and facilitates the complaint process for persons wanting to report a case of human trafficking.

United States Department of Justice: Trafficking in Persons and Worker Exploitation Task Force 1-888-428-7581

United States Department of Labor - assists with job-search; job-placement; job counseling; referrals to support services such as transportation, childcare, and housing. The

Wage and Hour Division also investigates complaints of labor law violation. According to a recent report titled, Human Trafficking: A Strategic Framework Could Help Enhance the Interagency Collaboration Needed to Effectively Combat Trafficking Crimes: 2007, indication was made that there were 139 trafficking cases prosecuted from October 1, 2004 through June 5, 2007, under the Trafficking Victims Protection Act (TVPA). There were 302 defendants convicted between 2001 and June 14, 2007 utilizing the TVPA. There were 228 sex trafficking defendants convicted and 74 labor trafficking defendants prosecuted. Prior to the TVPA, 67 defendants were convicted between 1995 and 2000. Of the defendants, twenty were for sex trafficking and forty-seven were for labor trafficking.

United States Department of State - coordinates international anti-trafficking programs and efforts.

State Assistance

Each law enforcement agency should consult with their State Attorney General to determine exactly what assistance is available in your state.

North Carolina Court System, Administrative Office of the Courts - list of available certified interpreters

Available certified Spanish interpreters -
http://www.nccourts.org/Citizens/CPrograms/Foreign/
Documents/directory.pdf

Available non-certified other language interpreters-
http://www.nccourts.org/Citizens/CPrograms/Foreign/
Documents/otherdirectory.pdf

North Carolina Department of Health and Human Services – victim benefits and temporary visas

> 325 N. Salisbury Street
> Raleigh, NC 27601
> 1-800-662-7030 (English/Espanol)
> http://www.dhhs.state.nc.us/

North Carolina Department of Health and Human Services - Services – Division of Social Services

> 325 N. Salisbury Street
> Raleigh, NC 27601
> (919) 733-3055
> http://www.dhhs.state.nc.us/dss/

North Carolina Department of Justice, Attorney General's Office – North Carolina Justice Academy (NCJA) – this is a state law enforcement training academy located in North Carolina and is funded by the North Carolina Department of Justice, Attorney General's Office. Their mission is to improve the quality and effectiveness of criminal justice services to the citizens of North Carolina through research, education, training, and support for criminal justice and related personnel. Resources available for any law enforcement agency include: instructional materials and delivery of developed law enforcement courses and technical assistance regarding the identification, investigation, and prosecution of human trafficking cases. The NCJA has a staff of experts and legal advisors that are available to answer questions regarding the crime of human trafficking.

> (910) 525-4151 or (828) 685-3600
> http://www.jus.state.nc.us/NCJA/

North Carolina Victim's Assistance Network – promotes the rights and needs of crime victims by providing information and referrals on over 1,500 victim service and criminal justice agencies, victim assistance programs, and advocacy groups.

P.O. Box 28557
Raleigh, NC 27611-8557
(919) 831-2857
1-800-348-5068
http://www.nc-van.org/

Chapter 6

Human Trafficking Laws and Related Crimes

*"No free government can survive that
is not based on the supremacy of law
where law ends, tyranny begins
law alone can give us freedom"*

*-As inscribed on the exterior of the United States
Department of Justice building in Washington D.C.*

The following statutes are offenses that may be related to the crime of human trafficking in North Carolina. Other state statutes may vary. Please consult with your state's Attorney General's Office for appropriate charges and updates to the statute.

North Carolina State Constitution Article I – Declaration of Rights Section 17. Slavery and involuntary servitude.

Slavery is forever prohibited. Involuntary servitude, except as a punishment for crime whereof the parties have been adjudged guilty, is forever prohibited.

North Carolina Criminal Laws :

NCGS § 14-39. Kidnapping.

(a)   Any person who shall unlawfully confine, restrain, or remove from one place to another, any other person 16 years of age or over without the consent of such person, or any other person under the age of 16 years without the consent of a parent or legal custodian of such person, shall be guilty of kidnapping if such confinement, restraint or removal is for the purpose of:

(1)   Holding such other person for a ransom or as a hostage or using such other person as a shield; or

(2)   Facilitating the commission of any felony or facilitating flight of any person following the commission of a felony; or

(3)   Doing serious bodily harm to or terrorizing the person so confined, restrained or removed or any other person; or

(4)   Holding such other person in involuntary servitude in violation of G.S. 14-43.12.

70

(5)   Trafficking another person with the intent that the other person be held in involuntary servitude or sexual servitude in violation of G.S. 14-43.11.

(6)   Subjecting or maintaining such other person for sexual servitude in violation of G.S. 14-43.13.

(b)   There shall be two degrees of kidnapping as defined by subsection (a). If the person kidnapped either was not released by the defendant in a safe place or had been seriously injured or sexually assaulted, the offense is kidnapping in the first degree and is punishable as a Class C felony. If the person kidnapped was released in a safe place by the defendant and had not been seriously injured or sexually assaulted, the offense is kidnapping in the second degree and is punishable as a Class E felony.

(c)   Any firm or corporation convicted of kidnapping shall be punished by a fine of not less than five thousand dollars ($5,000) nor more than one hundred thousand dollars ($100,000), and its charter and right to do business in the State of North Carolina shall be forfeited. (1933, c. 542; 1975, c. 843, s. 1; 1979, c. 760, s. 5; 1979, 2nd Sess., c. 1316, s. 47; 1981, c. 63, s. 1; c. 179, s. 14; 1983, c. 746, s. 2; 1993, c. 539, s. 1143; 1994, Ex. Sess., c. 24, s. 14(c); 1995, c. 509, s. 8; 2006-247, s. 20(c).)

71

NCGS § 14-40. Enticing minors out of the State for the purpose of employment.

If any person shall employ and carry beyond the limits of this State any minor, or shall induce any minor to go beyond the limits of this State, for the purpose of employment without the consent in writing, duly authenticated, of the parent, guardian or other person having authority over such minor, he shall be guilty of a Class 2 misdemeanor. The fact of the employment and going out of the State of the minor, or of the going out of the State by the minor, at the solicitation of the person for the purpose of employment, shall be prima facie evidence of knowledge that the person employed or solicited to go beyond the limits of the State is a minor. (1891, c. 45; Rev., s. 3630; C.S., s. 4222; 1969, c. 1224, s. 4; 1993, c. 539, s. 21; 1994, Ex. Sess., c. 24, s. 14(c).)

NCGS § 14-41. Abduction of children.

(a)   Any person who, without legal justification or defense, abducts or induces any minor child who is at least four years younger than the person to leave any person, agency, or institution lawfully entitled to the child's custody, placement, or care shall be guilty of a Class F felony.

(b)   The provisions of this section shall not apply to any public officer or employee in the performance of his or her duty. (1879, c. 81; Code, s. 973; Rev., s. 3358; C.S., s. 4223; 1979, c. 760, s. 5; 1979, 2nd Sess., c. 1316, s. 47; 1981, c. 63, s. 1; c. 179, s. 14; 1993, c. 539, s. 1144; 1994, Ex. Sess., c. 24, s. 14(c); 1995 (Reg. Sess., 1996), c. 745, s. 1.)

NCGS § 14-43.3. Felonious restraint.

A person commits the offense of felonious restraint if he unlawfully restrains another person without that person's consent, or the consent of the person's parent or legal custodian if the person is less than 16 years old, and moves the person from the place of the initial restraint by transporting him in a motor vehicle or other conveyance. Violation of this section is a Class F felony. Felonious restraint is considered a lesser included offense of kidnapping. (1985, c. 545, s. 1; 1993, c. 539, s. 1147; 1994, Ex. Sess., c. 24, s. 14(c).)

NCGS § 14-43.11. Human trafficking

(a)   A person commits the offense of human trafficking when that person knowingly recruits, entices, harbors, transports, provides, or obtains by any means another person with the intent that the other person be held in involuntary servitude or sexual servitude.

(b)   A person who violates this section is guilty of a Class F felony if the victim of the offense is an adult. A person who violates this section is guilty of a Class C felony if the victim of the offense is a minor.

(c)   Each violation of this section constitutes a separate offense and shall not merge with any other offense. Evidence of failure to deliver benefits or perform services standing alone shall not be sufficient to authorize a conviction under this section.

(d)   A person who is not a legal resident of North Carolina, and would consequently be ineligible for State public benefits or services, shall be eligible for the public benefits and services of any State agency if the person is otherwise eligible for the public benefit and is a victim of an offense charged under this section. Eligibility for public benefits and services shall terminate at such time as the victim's eligibility to remain in the United States is terminated under federal law. (2006-247, s. 20(b); 2007-547, s. 1.) (North Carolina General Statutes 2009)

NCGS § 14-43.12. Involuntary servitude.

(a)   A person commits the offense of involuntary servitude when that person knowingly and willfully holds another in involuntary servitude.

(b)   A person who violates this section is guilty of a Class F felony if the victim of the offense is an adult. A person who violates this section is guilty of a Class C felony if the victim of the offense is a minor.

(c)   Each violation of this section constitutes a separate offense and shall not merge with any other offense. Evidence of failure to deliver benefits or perform services standing alone shall not be sufficient to authorize a conviction under this section.

(d)   Nothing in this section shall be construed to affect the laws governing the relationship between an unemancipated minor and his or her parents or legal guardian.

(e)   If any person reports a violation of this section, which violation arises out of any contract for labor, to any party to the contract, the party shall immediately report the violation to the sheriff of the county in which the violation is alleged to have occurred for appropriate action. A person violating this subsection shall be guilty of a Class 1 misdemeanor. (1983, ch. 746, s. 1; 1993, c. 539, ss. 23, 1146; 1994, Ex. Sess., c. 24, s. 14(c); 2006-247, s. 20(b).) (North Carolina General Statutes 2009)

NCGS § 14-43.13. Sexual servitude.

(a)   A person commits the offense of sexual servitude when that person knowingly subjects or maintains another in sexual servitude.

(b)   A person who violates this section is guilty of a Class F felony if the victim of the offense is an adult. A person who violates this section is guilty of a Class C felony if the victim of the offense is a minor.

(c)   Each violation of this section constitutes a separate offense and shall not merge with any other offense. Evidence of failure to deliver benefits or perform services standing alone shall not be sufficient to authorize a conviction under this section. (2006-247, s. 20(b).) (North Carolina General Statutes 2009)

NCGS § 14-100. Obtaining property by false pretenses.

(a)   If any person shall knowingly and designedly by means of any kind of false pretense whatsoever, whether the false pretense is of a past or subsisting fact or of a future fulfillment or event, obtain or attempt to obtain from any person within this State

75

any money, goods, property, services, chose in action, or other thing of value with intent to cheat or defraud any person of such money, goods, property, services, chose in action or other thing of value, such person shall be guilty of a felony: Provided, that if, on the trial of anyone indicted for such crime, it shall be proved that he obtained the property in such manner as to amount to larceny or embezzlement, the jury shall have submitted to them such other felony proved; and no person tried for such felony shall be liable to be afterwards prosecuted for larceny or embezzlement upon the same facts: Provided, further, that it shall be sufficient in any indictment for obtaining or attempting to obtain any such money, goods, property, services, chose in action, or other thing of value by false pretenses to allege that the party accused did the act with intent to defraud, without alleging an intent to defraud any particular person, and without alleging any ownership of the money, goods, property, services, chose in action or other thing of value; and upon the trial of any such indictment, it shall not be necessary to prove either an intent to defraud any particular person or that the person to whom the false pretense was made was the person defrauded, but it shall be sufficient to allege and prove that the party accused made the false pretense charged with an intent to defraud. If the value of the money, goods, property, services, chose in action, or other thing of value is one hundred thousand dollars ($100,000) or more, a violation of this section is a Class C felony. If the value of the money, goods, property, services, chose in action, or other thing of value is less than one hundred thousand dollars ($100,000), a violation of this section is a Class H felony.

(b)   Evidence of nonfulfillment of a contract obligation standing alone shall not establish the essential element of intent to defraud.

(c)   For purposes of this section, "person" means person, association, consortium, corporation, body politic, partnership, or other group, entity, or organization. (33 Hen. VIII, c. 1, ss. 1, 2; 30 Geo. II, c. 24, s. 1; 1811, c. 814, s. 2, P.R.; R.C., c. 34, s. 67; Code, s. 1025; Rev., s. 3432; C.S., s. 4277; 1975, c. 783; 1979, c. 760, s. 5; 1979, 2nd Sess., c. 1316, s. 47;1981, c. 63, s. 1; c. 179, s. 14; 1997-443, s. 19.25(l).)

NCGS § 14-190.16. First degree sexual exploitation of a minor.

(a)   Offense. – A person commits the offense of first degree sexual exploitation of a minor if, knowing the character or content of the material or performance, he:

    (1)   Uses, employs, induces, coerces, encourages, or facilitates a minor to engage in or assist others to engage in sexual activity for a live performance or for the purpose of producing material that contains a visual representation depicting this activity; or

    (2)   Permits a minor under his custody or control to engage in sexual activity for a live performance or for the purpose of producing material that contains a visual representation depicting this activity; or

(3)   Transports or finances the transportation of a minor through or across this State with the intent that the minor engage in sexual activity for a live performance or for the purpose of producing material that contains a visual representation depicting this activity; or

(4)   Records, photographs, films, develops, or duplicates for sale or pecuniary gain material that contains a visual representation depicting a minor engaged in sexual activity.

(b)   Inference. – In a prosecution under this section, the trier of fact may infer that a participant in sexual activity whom material through its title, text, visual representations, or otherwise represents or depicts as a minor is a minor.

(c)   Mistake of Age. – Mistake of age is not a defense to a prosecution under this section.

(d)   Punishment and Sentencing. – Violation of this section is a Class C felony. (1985, c. 703, s. 9; 1993, c. 539, s. 1196; 1994, Ex. Sess., c. 24, s. 14(c); 1995, c. 507, s. 19.5(o); 2008-117, s. 3; 2008-218, s. 2.)

NCGS § 14-190.17. Second degree sexual exploitation of a minor.

(a)   Offense. – A person commits the offense of second degree sexual exploitation of a minor if, knowing the character or content of the material, he:

(1)   Records, photographs, films, develops, or duplicates material that contains a visual representation of a minor engaged in sexual activity; or

(2)   Distributes, transports, exhibits, receives, sells, purchases, exchanges, or solicits material that contains a visual representation of a minor engaged in sexual activity.

(b)   Inference. – In a prosecution under this section, the trier of fact may infer that a participant in sexual activity whom material through its title, text, visual representations or otherwise represents or depicts as a minor is a minor.

(c)   Mistake of Age. – Mistake of age is not a defense to a prosecution under this section.

(d)   Punishment and Sentencing. – Violation of this section is a Class E felony. (1985, c.   703, s. 9; 1993, c. 539, s. 1197; 1994, Ex. Sess., c. 24, s. 14(c); 2008-117, s. 4; 2008-218, s. 3.)

NCGS § 14-190.17A. Third degree sexual exploitation of a minor.

(a)   Offense. – A person commits the offense of third degree sexual exploitation of a minor if, knowing the character or content of the material, he possesses material that contains a visual representation of a minor engaging in sexual activity.

79

(b)   Inference. – In a prosecution under this section, the trier of fact may infer that a participant in sexual activity whom material through its title, text, visual representations or otherwise represents or depicts as a minor is a minor.

(c)   Mistake of Age. – Mistake of age is not a defense to a prosecution under this section.

(d)   Punishment and Sentencing. – Violation of this section is a Class H felony. (1989 (Reg. Sess., 1990), c. 1022, s. 1; 1993, c. 539, s. 1198; 1994, Ex. Sess., c. 24, s. 14(c); 2008-117, s. 5; 2008-218, s. 4.)

NCGS § 14-190.18. Promoting prostitution of a minor.

(a)   Offense. – A person commits the offense of promoting prostitution of a minor if he knowingly:

    (1)   Entices, forces, encourages, or otherwise facilitates a minor to participate in prostitution; or

    (2)   Supervises, supports, advises, or protects the prostitution of or by a minor.

(b)   Mistake of Age. – Mistake of age is not a defense to a prosecution under this section.

(c)   Punishment and Sentencing. – Violation of this section is a Class C felony. (1985, c. 703, s. 9; 1993, c. 539, s. 1199; 1994, Ex. Sess., c. 24, s. 14(c); 1995, c. 507, s. 19.5(p); 2008-117, s. 6.)

NCGS § 14-190.19. Participating in prostitution of a minor.

(a) Offense. – A person commits the offense of participating in the prostitution of a minor if he is not a minor and he patronizes a minor prostitute. As used in this section, "patronizing a minor prostitute" means:

    (1) Soliciting or requesting a minor to participate in prostitution;

    (2) Paying or agreeing to pay a minor, either directly or through the minor's agent, to participate in prostitution; or

    (3) Paying a minor, or the minor's agent, for having participated in prostitution, pursuant to a prior agreement.

(b) Mistake of Age. – Mistake of age is not a defense to a prosecution under this section.

(c) Punishment and Sentencing. – Violation of this section is a Class F felony. (1985, c. 703, s. 9; 1993, c. 539, s. 1200; 1994, Ex. Sess., c. 24, s. 14(c).)

NCGS § 14-202.1. Taking indecent liberties with children.

(a) A person is guilty of taking indecent liberties with children if, being 16 years of age or more and at least five years older than the child in question, he either:

(1)   Willfully takes or attempts to take any immoral, improper, or indecent liberties with any child of either sex under the age of 16 years for the purpose of arousing or gratifying sexual desire; or

(2)   Willfully commits or attempts to commit any lewd or lascivious act upon or with the body or any part or member of the body of any child of either sex under the age of 16 years.

(b)   Taking indecent liberties with children is punishable as a Class F felony. (1955, c. 764; 1975, c. 779; 1979, c. 760, s. 5; 1979, 2nd Sess., c. 1316, s. 47; 1981, c. 63, s. 1, c. 179, s. 14; 1993, c. 539, s. 1201; 1994, Ex. Sess., c. 24, s. 14(c).)

NCGS § 14-202.3. Solicitation of child by computer to commit an unlawful sex act.

(a)   Offense. – A person is guilty of solicitation of a child by a computer if the person is 16 years of age or older and the person knowingly, with the intent to commit an unlawful sex act, entices, advises, coerces, orders, or commands, by means of a computer, a child who is less than 16 years of age and at least 3 years younger than the defendant, or a person the defendant believes to be a child who is less than 16 years of age and who the defendant believes to be at least 3 years younger than the defendant, to meet with the defendant or any other person for the purpose of committing an unlawful sex act. Consent is not a defense to a charge under this section.

(b)   Jurisdiction. – The offense is committed in the State for purposes of determining jurisdiction, if the transmission that constitutes the offense either originates in the State or is received in the State.

(c)   Punishment. – A violation of this section is punishable as follows:

    (1)   A violation is a Class H felony except as provided by subdivision (2) of this subsection.

    (2)   If either the defendant, or any other person for whom the defendant was arranging the meeting in violation of this section, actually appears at the meeting location, then the violation is a Class G felony. (1995 (Reg. Sess., 1996), c. 632, s. 1; 2005-121, s. 1; 2008-218, s. 5.)

NCGS § 14-204. Prostitution and various acts abetting prostitution unlawful.

It shall be unlawful:

    (1)   To keep, set up, maintain, or operate any place, structure, building or conveyance for the purpose of prostitution or assignation.

    (2)   To occupy any place, structure, building, or conveyance for the purpose of prostitution or assignation; or for any person to permit any place, structure, building or conveyance owned by him or under his control to be used for the purpose of prostitution or assignation, with knowledge or reasonable

cause to know that the same is, or is to be, used for such purpose.

(3)   To receive, or to offer or agree to receive any person into any place, structure, building, or conveyance for the purpose of prostitution or assignation, or to permit any person to remain there for such purpose.

(4)   To direct, take, or transport, or to offer or agree to take or transport, any person to any place, structure, or building or to any other person, with knowledge or reasonable cause to know that the purpose of such directing, taking, or transporting is prostitution or assignation.

(5)   To procure, or to solicit, or to offer to procure or solicit for the purpose of prostitution or assignation.

(6)   To reside in, enter, or remain in any place, structure, or building, or to enter or remain in any conveyance, for the purpose of prostitution or assignation.

(7)   To engage in prostitution or assignation, or to aid or abet prostitution or assignation by any means whatsoever. (1919, c. 215, s. 1; C.S., s. 4358.)

North Carolina Civil Laws:

NCGS § 95-25.3. Minimum wage.

(a)   Every employer shall pay to each employee who in any workweek performs any work, wages of at least six dollars and fifteen cents ($6.15) per hour or the minimum wage set forth in paragraph 1 of section 6(a) of the Fair Labor Standards Act, 29 U.S.C. 206(a)(1), as that wage may change from time to time, whichever is higher, except as otherwise provided in this section.

(b)   In order to prevent curtailment of opportunities for employment, the wage rate for full-time students, learners, apprentices, and messengers, as defined under the Fair Labor Standards Act, shall be ninety percent (90%) of the rate in effect under subsection (a) above, rounded to the lowest nickel.

(c)   The Commissioner, in order to prevent curtailment of opportunities for employment, may, by regulation, establish a wage rate less than the wage rate in effect under section (a) which may apply to persons whose earning or productive capacity is impaired by age or physical or mental deficiency or injury, as such persons are defined under the Fair Labor Standards Act.

(d)   The Commissioner, in order to prevent curtailment of opportunities for employment of the economically disadvantaged and the unemployed, may, by regulation, establish a wage rate not less than eighty-five percent (85%) of the otherwise applicable wage rate in effect under subsection (a) which shall apply to all persons (i) who have been unemployed for at least 15 weeks and who are economically disadvantaged, or (ii) who are, or whose families are, receiving Work First Family Assistance or who are receiving supplemental security benefits under Title XVI of the Social Security Act.

Pursuant to regulations issued by the Commissioner, certificates establishing eligibility for such subminimum wage shall be issued by the Employment Security Commission.

The regulation issued by the Commissioner shall not permit employment at the subminimum rate for a period in excess of 52 weeks.

(e)   The Commissioner, in order to prevent curtailment of opportunities for employment, and to not adversely affect the viability of seasonal establishments, may, by regulation, establish a wage rate not less than eighty-five percent (85%) of the otherwise applicable wage rate in effect under subsection (a) which shall apply to any employee employed by an establishment which is a seasonal amusement or recreational establishment, or a seasonal food service establishment.

(f)   Tips earned by a tipped employee may be counted as wages only up to the amount permitted in section 3(m) of the Fair Labor Standards Act, 29 U.S.C. 203(m), if the tipped employee is notified in advance, is permitted to retain all tips and the employer maintains accurate and complete records of tips received by each employee as such tips are certified by the employee monthly or for each pay period. Even if the employee refuses to certify tips accurately, tips may still be counted as wages when the employer complies with the other requirements of this section and can demonstrate by monitoring tips that the employee regularly receives tips in the amount for which the credit is taken. Tip pooling shall also be permissible among employees who customarily and regularly receive tips; however, no employee's tips may be reduced by more than fifteen percent (15%) under a tip pooling arrangement.

(g)   Repealed by Session Laws 2006-259, s. 18, effective August 23, 2006. (1959, c. 475; 1963, c. 816; 1965, c. 229; 1969, c. 34, s. 1; 1971, c. 138; 1973, c. 802; 1975, c. 256, s. 1; 1977, c. 519; 1979, c. 839, s. 1; 1981, c. 493, s. 1; c. 663, s. 13; 1983, c. 708, s. 1; 1985, c. 97; 1987, c. 79; 1991, c. 270, ss. 1, 2; c. 330, s. 5; 1997-146, s. 1; 1997-443, s. 12.25; 2006-114, s. 1; 2006-259, s. 18.)

NCGS § 95-25.6. Wage payment.

Every employer shall pay every employee all wages and tips accruing to the employee on the regular payday. Pay periods may be daily, weekly, bi-weekly, semi-monthly, or monthly. Wages based upon bonuses, commissions, or other forms of calculation may be paid as infrequently as annually if prescribed in advance. (1975, c. 413, s. 3; 1977, c. 826, s. 3; 1979, c. 839, s. 1.)

NCGS § 95-25.8. Withholding of wages.

(a)   An employer may withhold or divert any portion of an employee's wages when:

(1)   The employer is required or empowered to do so by State or federal law;

(2)   When the amount or rate of the proposed deduction is known and agreed upon in advance, the employer must have written authorization from the employee which (i) is signed on or before the payday(s) for the pay period(s) from which the deduction is to be made; (ii) indicates the reason for the deduction; and (iii) states the actual dollar amount or percentage of wages which shall be deducted from one or more paychecks. Provided, that if the deduction is for the convenience of the employee, the employee shall be given a reasonable opportunity to withdraw the authorization; or

(3)   When the amount of the proposed deduction is not known and agreed upon in advance, the employer must have written authorization from the employee which (i) is signed on or before the payday(s) for the pay period(s) from which the deduction is to be made; and (ii) indicates the reason for the deduction. Prior to any deductions being made under this section, the employee must (i) receive advance written notice of the actual amount to be deducted; (ii) receive written notice of their right to withdraw the authorization; and (iii) be given a reasonable opportunity to withdraw the authorization in writing.

(b)   The withholding or diversion of wages owed for the employer's benefit must comply with the following requirements:

   (1)   In nonovertime workweeks, an employer may reduce wages to the minimum wage level.

   (2)   In overtime workweeks, employers may reduce wages to the minimum wage level for nonovertime hours.

   (3)   No reductions may be made to overtime wages owed.

(c)   In addition to complying with the requirements in subsections (a) and (b) of this section, an employer may withhold or divert a portion of an employee's wages for cash shortages, inventory shortages, or loss or damage to an employer's property after giving the employee written notice of the amount to be deducted seven days prior to the payday on which the deduction is to be made, except that when a separation occurs the seven-day notice is not required.

(d)   Notwithstanding subsections (a) and (b), above, an overpayment of wages to an employee as a result of a miscalculation or other bona fide error, advances of wages to an employee or to a third party at the employee's request, and the principal amount of loans made by an employer to an employee are considered prepayment of wages and may be withheld or deducted from an employee's wages. Deductions for interest and other charges related to loans by an employer to an employee shall require written authorization in accordance with subsection (a), above.

(e) Notwithstanding subsections (a) and (c), above, if criminal process has issued against an employee, an employee has been indicted, or an employee has been arrested pursuant to Articles 17, 20, and 32 of Chapter 15A of the General Statutes for a charge incident to a cash shortage, inventory shortage, or damage to an employer's property, an employer may withhold or divert a portion of the employee's wages in order to recoup the amount of the cash shortage, inventory shortage, or damage to the employer's property, without the written authorization required by this section, but the amount of such withholdings shall comply with the provisions of subsection (b) of this section. If the employee is not found guilty, then the amount deducted shall be reimbursed to the employee by the employer.

(f) For purposes of this section, a written authorization or written notice may be in the form of an electronic record in compliance with Article 40 of Chapter 66 (the Uniform Electronic Transactions Act).

(g) Nothing in this Article shall preclude an employer from bringing a civil action in the General Court of Justice to collect any amounts due the employer from the employee. (1975, c. 413, s. 6; 1979, c. 839, s. 1; 1981, c. 663, s. 2; 2005-453, s. 16.)

North Carolina Administrative Laws:

NCGS § 15A-832. Responsibilities of the District Attorney's Office.

(a)   Within 21 days after the arrest of the accused, but not less than 24 hours before the accused's first scheduled probable cause hearing, the district attorney's office shall provide to the victim a pamphlet or other written material that explains in a clear and concise manner the following:

   (1)   The victim's rights under this Article, including the right to confer with the attorney prosecuting the case about the disposition of the case and the right to provide a victim impact statement.

   (2)   The responsibilities of the district attorney's office under this Article.

   (3)   The victim's eligibility for compensation under the Crime Victims Compensation Act and the deadlines by which the victim must file a claim for compensation.

   (4)   The steps generally taken by the district attorney's office when prosecuting a felony case.

   (5)   Suggestions on what the victim should do if threatened or intimidated by the accused or someone acting on the accused's behalf.

   (6)   The name and telephone number of a victim and witness assistant in the district

attorney's office whom the victim may contact for further information.

(b)   Upon receiving the information in subsection (a) of this section, the victim shall, on a form provided by the district attorney's office, indicate whether the victim wishes to receive notices of some, all, or none of the trial and post trial proceedings involving the accused. If the victim elects to receive notices, the victim shall be responsible for notifying the district attorney's office or any other department or agency that has a responsibility under this Article of any changes in the victim's address and telephone number. The victim may alter the request for notification at any time by notifying the district attorney's office and completing the form provided by the district attorney's office.

(c)   The district attorney's office shall notify a victim of the date, time, and place of all trial court proceedings of the type that the victim has elected to receive notice. All notices required to be given by the district attorney's office shall be given in a manner that is reasonably calculated to be received by the victim prior to the date of the court proceeding.

(d)   Whenever practical, the district attorney's office shall provide a secure waiting area during court proceedings that does not place the victim in close proximity to the defendant or the defendant's family.

(e)   When the victim is to be called as a witness in a court proceeding, the court shall make every effort to permit the fullest attendance possible by the victim in the proceedings. This subsection shall not be construed to interfere with the defendant's right to a fair trial.

(f)   Prior to the disposition of the case, the district attorney's office shall offer the victim the opportunity to consult with the prosecuting attorney to obtain the views of the victim about the disposition of the case, including the victim's views about dismissal, plea or negotiations, sentencing, and any pretrial diversion programs.

(g)   At the sentencing hearing, the prosecuting attorney shall submit to the court a copy of a form containing the identifying information set forth in G.S. 15A-831(c) about any victim's electing to receive further notices under this Article. The clerk of superior court shall include the form with the final judgment and commitment, or judgment suspending sentence, transmitted to the Department of Correction or other agency receiving custody of the defendant and shall be maintained by the custodial agency as a confidential file.

(h)   When a person is a victim of a human trafficking offense and is entitled to benefits and services pursuant to G.S. 14-43.11(d), the district attorney's office shall so notify the Office of the Attorney General and Legal Aid of North Carolina, Inc., in addition to providing services under this Article. (1998-212, s. 19.4(c); 2001-433, s. 3; 2001-487, s. 120; 2007-547, s. 3.) (North Carolina General Statutes 2009)

NCGS § 15C-1. Purpose. Address Confidentiality Program.

The purpose of this Chapter is to enable the State and the agencies of North Carolina to respond to requests for public records without disclosing the location of a victim of domestic violence, sexual offense, stalking, or human trafficking; to enable interagency cooperation in providing address confidentiality for victims of domestic violence, sexual offense, stalking, or human trafficking; and to enable the State and its agencies to accept a program participant's use of an address designated by the Office of the Attorney General as a substitute address. (2002-171, s. 1; 2007-547, s. 4.) (North Carolina General Statutes 2009)

NCGS § 15C-2. Definitions.

The following definitions apply in this Chapter:

(1)   Actual address or address. – A residential, work, or school street address as specified on the individual's application to be a program participant under this Chapter.

(2)   Address Confidentiality Program or Program. – A program in the Office of the Attorney General to protect the confidentiality of the address of a relocated victim of domestic violence, sexual offense, or stalking to prevent the victim's assailants or potential assailants from finding the victim through public records.

(3)   Agency of North Carolina or agency. – Includes every elected or appointed State or local public office, public officer, or official; institution, board, commission, bureau, council, department, authority, or other unit of government of the State or of any local government; or

unit, special district, or other political subdivision of State or local government.

(4)   Application assistant. – An employee of an agency or nonprofit organization who provides counseling, referral, shelter, or other specialized services to victims of domestic violence, sexual offense, stalking, or human trafficking and who has been designated by the Attorney General to assist individuals with applications to participate in the Address Confidentiality Program.

(5)   Attorney General. – Office of the Attorney General.

(6)   Person. – Any individual, corporation, limited liability company, partnership, trust, estate, or other association or any state, the United States, or any subdivision thereof.

(7)   Program participant. – An individual accepted into the Address Confidentiality Program in accordance with this Chapter.

(8)   Public record. – A public record as defined in Chapter 132 of the General Statutes.

(9)   Substitute address. – An address designated by the Attorney General under the Address Confidentiality Program.

(10)   Victim of domestic violence. – An individual against whom domestic violence, as described in G.S. 50B-1, has been committed.

(11)   Victim of a sexual offense. – An individual against whom a sexual offense, as described in Article 7A of

Chapter 14 of the General Statutes, has been committed.

(12)   Victim of stalking. – An individual against whom stalking, as described in G.S. 14-277.3, has been committed.

(13)   Victim of human trafficking. – An individual against whom human trafficking, as described in G.S. 14-43.11, has been committed. (2002-171, s. 1; 2007-547, s. 5.)   (North Carolina General Statutes 2009)

NCGS § 15C-3. Address Confidentiality Program.

The General Assembly establishes the Address Confidentiality Program in the Office of the Attorney General to protect the confidentiality of the address of a relocated victim of domestic violence, sexual offense, stalking, or human trafficking to prevent the victim's assailants or potential assailants from finding the victim through public records. Under this Program, the Attorney General shall designate a substitute address for a program participant and act as the agent of the program participant for purposes of service of process and receiving and forwarding first-class mail or certified or registered mail. The Attorney General shall not be required to forward any mail other than first-class mail or certified or registered mail to the program participant. The Attorney General shall not be required to track or otherwise maintain records of any mail received on behalf of a program participant unless the mail is certified or registered mail. (2002-171, s. 1; 2007-547, s. 6.) (North Carolina General Statutes 2009)

NCGS § 15C-10. Assistance for Program Applicants.

(a)   The Attorney General shall designate agencies of North Carolina and nonprofit organizations that provide counseling and shelter services to victims of domestic violence, sexual offense, stalking, or human trafficking to assist individuals applying to be program participants. Any assistance and counseling rendered by the Office of the Attorney General or its designee to applicants shall in no way be construed as legal advice.

(b)   The Attorney General, upon receiving notification pursuant to G.S. 15A-832(h), shall, within 96 hours of receiving the notification, issue the victim a letter of certification of eligibility or other relevant document entitling the person to have access to State benefits and services. (2002-171, s. 1; 2007-547, s. 8.)

Federal Laws:

U.S. Constitution Amendment Thirteen

Section 1.

Neither slavery nor involuntary servitude, except as a punishment for crime whereof the party shall have been duly convicted, shall exist within the United States, or any place subject to their jurisdiction.

Section 2.

Congress shall have power to enforce this article by appropriate legislation.

Federal Criminal Laws:

18 U.S.C. § 1201. Kidnapping.

(a)   Whoever unlawfully seizes, confines, inveigles, decoys, kidnaps, abducts, or carries away and holds for ransom or reward or otherwise any person, except in the case of a minor by the parent thereof, when—

    (1)   the person is willfully transported in interstate or foreign commerce, regardless of whether the person was alive when transported across a State boundary, or the offender travels in interstate or foreign commerce or uses the mail or any means, facility, or instrumentality of interstate or foreign commerce in committing or in furtherance of the commission of the offense;

    (2)   any such act against the person is done within the special maritime and territorial jurisdiction of the United States;

    (3)   any such act against the person is done within the special aircraft jurisdiction of the United States as defined in section 46501 of title 49;

    (4)   the person is a foreign official, an internationally protected person, or an official guest as those terms are defined in section 1116 (b) of this title; or

(5)   the person is among those officers and employees described in section 1114 of this title and any such act against the person is done while the person is engaged in, or on account of, the performance of official duties, shall be punished by imprisonment for any term of years or for life and, if the death of any person results, shall be punished by death or life imprisonment.

(b)   With respect to subsection (a)(1), above, the failure to release the victim within twenty-four hours after he shall have been unlawfully seized, confined, inveigled, decoyed, kidnapped, abducted, or carried away shall create a rebuttable presumption that such person has been transported in interstate or foreign commerce. Notwithstanding the preceding sentence, the fact that the presumption under this section has not yet taken effect does not preclude a Federal investigation of a possible violation of this section before the 24-hour period has ended.

(c)   If two or more persons conspire to violate this section and one or more of such persons do any overt act to effect the object of the conspiracy, each shall be punished by imprisonment for any term of years or for life.

(d)   Whoever attempts to violate subsection (a) shall be punished by imprisonment for not more than twenty years.

(e)   If the victim of an offense under subsection (a) is an internationally protected person outside the United States, the United States may exercise jurisdiction over the offense if

(1)   the victim is a representative, officer, employee, or agent of the United States,

(2)   an offender is a national of the United States, or

(3)   an offender is afterwards found in the United States. As used in this subsection, the United States includes all areas under the jurisdiction of the United States including any of the places within the provisions of sections 5 and 7 of this title and section 46501 (2) of title 49. For purposes of this subsection, the term "national of the United States" has the meaning prescribed in section 101(a)(22) of the Immigration and Nationality Act (8 U.S.C. 1101 (a)(22)).

(f)   In the course of enforcement of subsection (a)(4) and any other sections prohibiting a conspiracy or attempt to violate subsection (a)(4), the Attorney General may request assistance from any Federal, State, or local agency, including the Army, Navy, and Air Force, any statute, rule, or regulation to the contrary notwithstanding.

(g)   Special Rule for Certain Offenses Involving Children.—

(1)   To whom applicable.— If—

(A) the victim of an offense under this section has not attained the age of eighteen years; and

      (B)   the offender—

          (i)   has attained such age; and

          (ii)   is not—

              (I)   a parent;

              (II)   a grandparent;

              (III)   a brother;

              (IV)   a sister;

              (V)   an aunt;

              (VI)   an uncle; or

              (VII) an individual having legal custody of the victim;
the sentence under this section for such offense shall include imprisonment for not less than 20 years. [(2) Repealed. Pub. L. 108–21, title I, § 104(b), Apr. 30, 2003, 117 Stat. 653.]

  (h)   As used in this section, the term "parent" does not include a person whose parental rights with respect to the victim of an offense under this section have been terminated by a final court order.

18 U.S.C. § 1546. Fraud and misuse of visas, permits, and other documents.

(a) Whoever knowingly forges, counterfeits, alters, or falsely makes any immigrant or nonimmigrant visa, permit, border crossing card, alien registration receipt card, or other document prescribed by statute or regulation for entry into or as evidence of authorized stay or employment in the United States, or utters, uses, attempts to use, possesses, obtains, accepts, or receives any such visa, permit, border crossing card, alien registration receipt card, or other document prescribed by statute or regulation for entry into or as evidence of authorized stay or employment in the United States, knowing it to be forged, counterfeited, altered, or falsely made, or to have been procured by means of any false claim or statement, or to have been otherwise procured by fraud or unlawfully obtained; or

Whoever, except under direction of the Attorney General or the Commissioner of the Immigration and Naturalization Service, or other proper officer, knowingly possesses any blank permit, or engraves, sells, brings into the United States, or has in his control or possession any plate in the likeness of a plate designed for the printing of permits, or makes any print, photograph, or impression in the likeness of any immigrant or nonimmigrant visa, permit or other document required for entry into the United States, or has in his possession a distinctive paper which has been adopted by the Attorney General or the Commissioner of the Immigration and

102

Naturalization Service for the printing of such visas, permits, or documents; or

Whoever, when applying for an immigrant or nonimmigrant visa, permit, or other document required for entry into the United States, or for admission to the United States personates another, or falsely appears in the name of a deceased individual, or evades or attempts to evade the immigration laws by appearing under an assumed or fictitious name without disclosing his true identity, or sells or otherwise disposes of, or offers to sell or otherwise dispose of, or utters, such visa, permit, or other document, to any person not authorized by law to receive such document; or

Whoever knowingly makes under oath, or as permitted under penalty of perjury under section 1746 of title 28, United States Code, knowingly subscribes as true, any false statement with respect to a material fact in any application, affidavit, or other document required by the immigration laws or regulations prescribed thereunder, or knowingly presents any such application, affidavit, or other document which contains any such false statement or which fails to contain any reasonable basis in law or fact—

Shall be fined under this title or imprisoned not more than 25 years (if the offense was committed to facilitate an act of international terrorism (as defined in section 2331 of this title)), 20 years (if the offense was committed to facilitate a drug trafficking crime (as defined in section 929 (a) of this title)), 10 years (in the case of the first or second such offense, if the offense was not committed to facilitate such an act of international terrorism or a drug trafficking crime), or 15 years (in the case of any other offense), or both.

(b)   Whoever uses—

(1)   an identification document, knowing (or having reason to know) that the document was not issued lawfully for the use of the possessor,

(2)   an identification document knowing (or having reason to know) that the document is false, or

(3)   a false attestation, for the purpose of satisfying a requirement of section 274A(b) of the Immigration and Nationality Act, shall be fined under this title, imprisoned not more than 5 years, or both.

(c)   This section does not prohibit any lawfully authorized investigative, protective, or intelligence activity of a law enforcement agency of the United States, a State, or a subdivision of a State, or of an intelligence agency of the United States, or any activity authorized under title V of the Organized Crime Control Act of 1970 (18 U.S.C. note prec. 3481).[1] For purposes of this section, the term "State" means a State of the United States, the District of Columbia, and any commonwealth, territory, or possession of the United States.

18 U.S.C. § 1581. Peonage; obstructing enforcement.

(a)   Whoever holds or returns any person to a condition of peonage, or arrests any person with the intent of placing him in or returning him to a condition of peonage, shall be fined under this title or imprisoned not more than 20 years, or both. If death results from the violation of this section, or if the violation includes kidnapping or an attempt to kidnap, aggravated sexual abuse or the attempt to commit aggravated sexual abuse, or an attempt to kill, the defendant shall be fined under this title or imprisoned for any term of years or life, or both.

(b)   Whoever obstructs, or attempts to obstruct, or in any way interferes with or prevents the enforcement of this section, shall be liable to the penalties prescribed in subsection (a).

18 U.S.C. § 1582. Vessels for slave trade.

Whoever, whether as master, factor, or owner, builds, fits out, equips, loads, or otherwise prepares or sends away any vessel, in any port or place within the United States, or causes such vessel to sail from any such port or place, for the purpose of procuring any person from any foreign kingdom or country to be transported and held, sold, or otherwise disposed of as a slave, or held to service or labor, shall be fined under this title or imprisoned not more than seven years, or both.

18 U.S.C. § 1583. Enticement into slavery.

Whoever kidnaps or carries away any other person, with the intent that such other person be sold into involuntary servitude, or held as a slave; or

Whoever entices, persuades, or induces any other person to go on board any vessel or to any other place with the intent that he may be made or held as a slave, or sent out of the country to be so made or held—

Shall be fined under this title or imprisoned not more than 20 years, or both. If death results from the violation of this section, or if the violation includes kidnapping or an attempt to kidnap, aggravated sexual abuse or the attempt to commit aggravated sexual abuse, or an attempt to kill, the defendant shall be fined under this title or imprisoned for any term of years or life, or both.

18 U.S.C. § 1584. Sale into involuntary servitude.

Whoever knowingly and willfully holds to involuntary servitude or sells into any condition of involuntary servitude, any other person for any term, or brings within the United States any person so held, shall be fined under this title or imprisoned not more than 20 years, or both. If death results from the violation of this section, or if the violation includes kidnapping or an attempt to kidnap, aggravated sexual abuse or the attempt to commit aggravated sexual abuse, or an attempt to kill, the defendant shall be fined under this title or imprisoned for any term of years or life, or both.

18 U.S.C. § 1585. Seizure, detention, transportation or sale of slaves.

Whoever, being a citizen or resident of the United States and a member of the crew or ship's company of any foreign vessel engaged in the slave trade, or whoever, being of the crew or ship's company of any vessel owned in whole or in part, or navigated for, or in behalf of, any citizen of the United States, lands from such vessel, and on any foreign shore seizes any person with intent to make that person a slave, or decoys, or forcibly brings, carries, receives, confines, detains or transports any person as a slave on board such vessel, or, on board such vessel, offers or attempts to sell any such person as a slave, or on the high seas or anywhere on tide water, transfers or delivers to any other vessel any such person with intent to make such person a slave, or lands or delivers on shore from such vessel any person with intent to sell, or having previously sold, such person as a slave, shall be fined under this title or imprisoned not more than seven years, or both.

18 U.S.C. § 1586. Service on vessels in slave trade.

Whoever, being a citizen or resident of the United States, voluntarily serves on board of any vessel employed or made use of in the transportation of slaves from any foreign country or place to another, shall be fined under this title or imprisoned not more than two years, or both.

18 U.S.C. § 1587. Possession of slaves aboard vessel.

Whoever, being the captain, master, or commander of any vessel found in any river, port, bay, harbor, or on the high seas within the jurisdiction of the United States, or hovering off the coast thereof, and having on board any person for the purpose of selling such person as a slave, or with intent to land such person for such purpose, shall be fined under this title or imprisoned not more than four years, or both.

18 U.S.C. § 1588. Transportation of slaves from United States.

Whoever, being the master or owner or person having charge of any vessel, receives on board any other person with the knowledge or intent that such person is to be carried from any place within the United States to any other place to be held or sold as a slave, or carries away from any place within the United States any such person with the intent that he may be so held or sold as a slave, shall be fined under this title or imprisoned not more than 10 years, or both.

18 U.S.C. § 1589. Forced labor.

Whoever knowingly provides or obtains the labor or services of a person—

(1)   by threats of serious harm to, or physical restraint against, that person or another person;

(2)   by means of any scheme, plan, or pattern intended to cause the person to believe that, if the person did not perform such labor or services, that person or another person would suffer serious harm or physical restraint; or

(3)   by means of the abuse or threatened abuse of law or the legal process,
shall be fined under this title or imprisoned not more than 20 years, or both. If death results from the violation of this section, or if the violation includes kidnapping or an attempt to kidnap, aggravated sexual abuse or the attempt to commit aggravated sexual abuse, or an attempt to kill, the defendant shall be fined under this title or imprisoned for any term of years or life, or both.

18 U.S.C. § 1590. Trafficking with respect to peonage, slavery, involuntary servitude, or forced labor.

Whoever knowingly recruits, harbors, transports, provides, or obtains by any means, any person for labor or services in violation of this chapter shall be fined under this title or imprisoned not more than 20 years, or both. If death results from the violation of this section, or if the violation includes kidnapping or an attempt to kidnap, aggravated sexual abuse, or the attempt to commit aggravated sexual abuse, or an attempt to kill, the defendant shall be fined under this title or imprisoned for any term of years or life, or both.

18 U.S.C. § 1591. Sex trafficking of children or by force, fraud, or coercion.

    (a)   Whoever knowingly—

        (1)   in or affecting interstate or foreign commerce, or within the special maritime and territorial jurisdiction of the United States, recruits, entices, harbors, transports, provides, or obtains by any means a person; or

        (2)   benefits, financially or by receiving anything of value, from participation in a venture which has engaged in an act described in violation of paragraph (1), knowing that force, fraud, or coercion described in subsection (c)(2) will be used to cause the person to engage in a commercial sex act, or that the person has not attained the age of 18 years and will be caused to engage in a commercial sex act, shall be punished as provided in subsection (b).

    (b)   The punishment for an offense under subsection (a) is—

(1)   if the offense was effected by force, fraud, or coercion or if the person recruited, enticed, harbored, transported, provided, or obtained had not attained the age of 14 years at the time of such offense, by a fine under this title and imprisonment for any term of years not less than 15 or for life; or

(2)   if the offense was not so effected, and the person recruited, enticed, harbored, transported, provided, or obtained had attained the age of 14 years but had not attained the age of 18 years at the time of such offense, by a fine under this title and imprisonment for not less than 10 years or for life.

(c)   In this section:

(1)   The term "commercial sex act" means any sex act, on account of which anything of value is given to or received by any person.

(2)   The term "coercion" means—

(A)   threats of serious harm to or physical restraint against any person;

(B)   any scheme, plan, or pattern intended to cause a person to believe that failure to perform an act would result in serious harm to or physical restraint against any person; or

(C)   the abuse or threatened abuse of law or the legal process.

(3)   The term "venture" means any group of two or more individuals associated in fact, whether or not a legal entity.

18 U.S.C. § 1592. Unlawful conduct with respect to documents in furtherance of trafficking, peonage, slavery, involuntary servitude, or forced labor.

(a)   Whoever knowingly destroys, conceals, removes, confiscates, or possesses any actual or purported passport or other immigration document, or any other actual or purported government identification document, of another person—

(1)   in the course of a violation of section 1581, 1583, 1584, 1589, 1590, 1591, or 1594 (a);

(2)   with intent to violate section 1581, 1583, 1584, 1589, 1590, or 1591; or

(3)   to prevent or restrict or to attempt to prevent or restrict, without lawful authority, the person's liberty to move or travel, in order to maintain the labor or services of that person, when the person is or has been a victim of a severe form of trafficking in persons, as defined in section 103 of the

111

Trafficking Victims Protection Act of 2000, shall be fined under this title or imprisoned for not more than 5 years, or both.

(b) Subsection (a) does not apply to the conduct of a person who is or has been a victim of a severe form of trafficking in persons, as defined in section 103 of the Trafficking Victims Protection Act of 2000, if that conduct is caused by, or incident to, that trafficking.

18 U.S.C. § 1962. Racketeer influenced and corrupt organizations.

(a) It shall be unlawful for any person who has received any income derived, directly or indirectly, from a pattern of racketeering activity or through collection of an unlawful debt in which such person has participated as a principal within the meaning of section 2, title 18, United States Code, to use or invest, directly or indirectly, any part of such income, or the proceeds of such income, in acquisition of any interest in, or the establishment or operation of, any enterprise which is engaged in, or the activities of which affect, interstate or foreign commerce. A purchase of securities on the open market for purposes of investment, and without the intention of controlling or participating in the control of the issuer, or of assisting another to do so, shall not be unlawful under this subsection if the securities of the issuer held by the purchaser, the members of his immediate family, and his or their accomplices in any pattern or racketeering

112

activity or the collection of an unlawful debt after such purchase do not amount in the aggregate to one percent of the outstanding securities of any one class, and do not confer, either in law or in fact, the power to elect one or more directors of the issuer.

(b)   It shall be unlawful for any person through a pattern of racketeering activity or through collection of an unlawful debt to acquire or maintain, directly or indirectly, any interest in or control of any enterprise which is engaged in, or the activities of which affect, interstate or foreign commerce.

(c)   It shall be unlawful for any person employed by or associated with any enterprise engaged in, or the activities of which affect, interstate or foreign commerce, to conduct or participate, directly or indirectly, in the conduct of such enterprise's affairs through a pattern of racketeering activity or collection of unlawful debt.

(d)   It shall be unlawful for any person to conspire to violate any of the provisions of subsection (a), (b), or (c) of this section.

18 U.S.C. § 2251. Sexual exploitation of children.

(a)   Any person who employs, uses, persuades, induces, entices, or coerces any minor to engage in, or who has a minor assist any other person to engage in, or who transports any minor in interstate or foreign commerce, or in any Territory or Possession of the United

113

States, with the intent that such minor engage in, any sexually explicit conduct for the purpose of producing any visual depiction of such conduct, shall be punished as provided under subsection (e), if such person knows or has reason to know that such visual depiction will be transported in interstate or foreign commerce or mailed, if that visual depiction was produced using materials that have been mailed, shipped, or transported in interstate or foreign commerce by any means, including by computer, or if such visual depiction has actually been transported in interstate or foreign commerce or mailed.

(b)   Any parent, legal guardian, or person having custody or control of a minor who knowingly permits such minor to engage in, or to assist any other person to engage in, sexually explicit conduct for the purpose of producing any visual depiction of such conduct shall be punished as provided under subsection (e) of this section, if such parent, legal guardian, or person knows or has reason to know that such visual depiction will be transported in interstate or foreign commerce or mailed, if that visual depiction was produced using materials that have been mailed, shipped, or transported in interstate or foreign commerce by any means, including by computer, or if such visual depiction has actually been transported in interstate or foreign commerce or mailed.

(c) (1) Any person who, in a circumstance described in paragraph (2), employs, uses, persuades, induces, entices, or coerces any minor to engage in, or who has a minor assist any other person to engage in, any sexually explicit conduct outside of the United States, its territories or possessions, for the purpose of producing any visual depiction of such conduct, shall be punished as provided under subsection (e).

(c)(2) The circumstance referred to in paragraph (1) is that—

   (A)   the person intends such visual depiction to be transported to the United States, its territories or possessions, by any means, including by computer or mail; or

   (B)   the person transports such visual depiction to the United States, its territories or possessions, by any means, including by computer or mail.

(d)   In this section:

   (1)   Any person who, in a circumstance described in paragraph (2), knowingly makes, prints, or publishes, or causes to be made, printed, or published, any notice or advertisement seeking or offering—

      (A)   to receive, exchange, buy, produce, display, distribute, or reproduce, any visual depiction, if the production of such visual depiction involves the use of a minor engaging in sexually explicit conduct and such visual depiction is of such conduct; or

(B)   participation in any act of sexually explicit conduct by or with any minor for the purpose of producing a visual depiction of such conduct; shall be punished as provided under subsection (e).

(2)   The circumstance referred to in paragraph (1) is that—

(A)   such person knows or has reason to know that such notice or advertisement will be transported in interstate or foreign commerce by any means including by computer or mailed; or

(B)   such notice or advertisement is transported in interstate or foreign commerce by any means including by computer or mailed.

(e)   Any individual who violates, or attempts or conspires to violate, this section shall be fined under this title and imprisoned not less than 15 years nor more than 30 years, but if such person has one prior conviction under this chapter, section 1591, chapter 71section 1591, chapter 71, chapter 109A, or chapter 117, or under section 920 of title 10 (article 120 of the Uniform Code of Military Justice), or under the laws of any State relating to aggravated sexual abuse, sexual abuse, abusive sexual contact involving a minor or ward, or sex trafficking of children, or the production, possession, receipt, mailing, sale, distribution, shipment, or transportation of child pornography, such person shall be fined under this title and imprisoned for not less than 25 years nor more than 50 years, but if such person has 2 or more prior convictions under this chapter, chapter 71, chapter 109A, or chapter 117, or under section 920 of title 10 (article 120 of the Uniform Code of Military Justice), or under the laws of any State relating to the sexual exploitation of children, such person shall be fined under this title and imprisoned not less than 35 years nor more than life. Any organization that violates, or attempts or conspires to violate, this section shall be fined under this title. Whoever, in the course of an offense under this section, engages in conduct that results in the death of a person, shall be punished by death or imprisoned for not less than 30 years or for life.

18 U.S.C. § 2251A. Selling or buying of children

(a)   Any parent, legal guardian, or other person having custody or control of a minor who sells or otherwise transfers custody or control of such minor, or offers to sell or otherwise transfer custody of such minor either—

(1)	with knowledge that, as a consequence of the sale or transfer, the minor will be portrayed in a visual depiction engaging in, or assisting another person to engage in, sexually explicit conduct; or

(2)	with intent to promote either—

(A)	the engaging in of sexually explicit conduct by such minor for the purpose of producing any visual depiction of such conduct; or

(B)	the rendering of assistance by the minor to any other person to engage in sexually explicit conduct for the purpose of producing any visual depiction of such conduct; shall be punished by imprisonment for not less than 30 years or for life and by a fine under this title, if any of the circumstances described in subsection (c) of this section exist.

(b)	Whoever purchases or otherwise obtains custody or control of a minor, or offers to purchase or otherwise obtain custody or control of a minor either—

(1)	with knowledge that, as a consequence of the purchase or obtaining of custody, the minor will be portrayed in a visual depiction engaging in, or assisting

118

another person to engage in, sexually explicit conduct; or

(2)   with intent to promote either—

     (A)   the engaging in of sexually explicit conduct by such minor for the purpose of producing any visual depiction of such conduct; or

     (B)   the rendering of assistance by the minor to any other person to engage in sexually explicit conduct for the purpose of producing any visual depiction of such conduct; shall be punished by imprisonment for not less than 30 years or for life and by a fine under this title, if any of the circumstances described in subsection (c) of this section exist.

(c)   The circumstances referred to in subsections (a) and (b) are that—

     (1)   in the course of the conduct described in such subsections the minor or the actor traveled in or was transported in interstate or foreign commerce;

     (2)   any offer described in such subsections was communicated or transported in interstate or foreign commerce by any

means including by computer or mail; or

(3)   the conduct described in such subsections took place in any territory or possession of the United States.

18 U.S.C. § 2421. Transportation for illegal sexual activity and related crimes.

Whoever knowingly transports any individual in interstate or foreign commerce, or in any Territory or Possession of the United States, with intent that such individual engage in prostitution, or in any sexual activity for which any person can be charged with a criminal offense, or attempts to do so, shall be fined under this title or imprisoned not more than 10 years, or both.

Federal Civil Laws:

18 U.S.C. § 1595. Trafficking Victims Protection Act – private right of action.

(a)   An individual who is a victim of a violation of section 1589, 1590, or 1591 of this chapter may bring a civil action against the perpetrator in an appropriate district court of the United States and may recover damages and reasonable attorneys fees.

(b)   In this section:

(1)   Any civil action filed under this section shall be stayed during the pendency of any criminal action arising out of the

same occurrence in which the claimant is the victim.

(2) In this subsection, a "criminal action" includes investigation and prosecution and is pending until final adjudication in the trial court.

18 U.S.C. § 1964. Racketeer influenced and corrupt organizations (civil remedy).

(a) The district courts of the United States shall have jurisdiction to prevent and restrain violations of section 1962 of this chapter by issuing appropriate orders, including, but not limited to: ordering any person to divest himself of any interest, direct or indirect, in any enterprise; imposing reasonable restrictions on the future activities or investments of any person, including, but not limited to, prohibiting any person from engaging in the same type of endeavor as the enterprise engaged in, the activities of which affect interstate or foreign commerce; or ordering dissolution or reorganization of any enterprise, making due provision for the rights of innocent persons.

(b) The Attorney General may institute proceedings under this section. Pending final determination thereof, the court may at any time enter such restraining orders or prohibitions, or take such other actions, including the acceptance of satisfactory performance bonds, as it shall deem proper.

(c) Any person injured in his business or property by reason of a violation of section 1962 of this chapter may sue therefore in any appropriate United States district court and shall recover threefold the damages he sustains and the cost of the suit, including a reasonable attorney's fee, except that no person may rely upon any conduct that would have been actionable as fraud in the purchase or sale of securities to establish a violation of section 1962. The exception contained in the preceding sentence does not apply to an action against any person that is criminally convicted in connection with the fraud, in which case the statute of limitations shall start to run on the date on which the conviction becomes final.

(d) A final judgment or decree rendered in favor of the United States in any criminal proceeding brought by the United States under this chapter shall stop the defendant from denying the essential allegations of the criminal offense in any subsequent civil proceeding brought by the United States.

22 U.S.C. § 7101 Trafficking Victims Protection Act.

(1) The United States has demonstrated international leadership in combating human trafficking and slavery through the enactment of the Trafficking Victims Protection Act of 2000 (division A of Public Law 106–386; 22 U.S.C. 7101 et seq.) and the Trafficking Victims Protection Reauthorization Act of 2003 (Public Law 108–193) [see Short Title of 2003 Amendment note above].

(2)   The United States Government currently estimates that 600,000 to 800,000 individuals are trafficked across international borders each year and exploited through forced labor and commercial sex exploitation. An estimated 80 percent of such individuals are women and girls.

(3)   Since the enactment of the Trafficking Victims Protection Act of 2000 [Oct. 28, 2000], United States efforts to combat trafficking in persons have focused primarily on the international trafficking in persons, including the trafficking of foreign citizens into the United States.

(4)   Trafficking in persons also occurs within the borders of a country, including the United States.

(5)   No known studies exist that quantify the problem of trafficking in children for the purpose of commercial sexual exploitation in the United States. According to a report issued by researchers at the University of Pennsylvania in 2001, as many as 300,000 children in the United States are at risk for commercial sexual exploitation, including trafficking, at any given time.

(6)   Runaway and homeless children in the United States are highly susceptible to being domestically trafficked for commercial sexual exploitation. According to the National Runaway Switchboard, every day in the United States, between 1,300,000 and 2,800,000 runaway and homeless youth live on the streets. One out of every seven children will run away from home before the age of 18.

(7)   Following armed conflicts and during humanitarian emergencies, indigenous populations face increased

security challenges and vulnerabilities which result in myriad forms of violence, including trafficking for sexual and labor exploitation. Foreign policy and foreign aid professionals increasingly recognize the increased activity of human traffickers in post-conflict settings and during humanitarian emergencies.

(8)   There is a need to protect populations in post-conflict settings and humanitarian emergencies from being trafficked for sexual or labor exploitation. The efforts of aid agencies to address the protection needs of, among others, internally displaced persons and refugees are useful in this regard. Nonetheless, there is a need for further integrated programs and strategies at the United States Agency for International Development, the Department of State, and the Department of Defense to combat human trafficking, including through protection and prevention methodologies, in post-conflict environments and during humanitarian emergencies.

(9)   International and human rights organizations have documented a correlation between international deployments of military and civilian peacekeepers and aid workers and a resulting increase in the number of women and girls trafficked into prostitution in post-conflict regions.

(10)   The involvement of employees and contractors of the United States Government and members of the Armed Forces in trafficking in persons, facilitating the trafficking in persons, or exploiting the victims of trafficking in persons is inconsistent with United States laws and policies and undermines the credibility and mission of United States Government programs in post-conflict regions.

(11)   Further measures are needed to ensure that United States Government personnel and contractors are held accountable for involvement with acts of trafficking in persons, including by expanding United States criminal jurisdiction to all United States Government contractors abroad."

Pub. L. 108–193, § 2, Dec. 19, 2003, 117 Stat. 2875, provided that: "Congress finds the following:

"(1)   Trafficking in persons continues to victimize countless men, women, and children in the United States and abroad.

(2)   Since the enactment of the Trafficking Victims Protection Act of 2000 (division A of Public Law 106–386) [see Short Title note above], the United States Government has made significant progress in investigating and prosecuting acts of trafficking and in responding to the needs of victims of trafficking in the United States and abroad.

(3)   On the other hand, victims of trafficking have faced unintended obstacles in the process of securing needed assistance, including admission to the United States under section 101(a)(15)(T)(i) of the Immigration and Nationality Act [8 U.S.C. 1101 (a)(15)(T)(i)].

(4)   Additional research is needed to fully understand the phenomenon of trafficking in persons and to determine the most effective strategies for combating trafficking in persons.

(5)   Corruption among foreign law enforcement authorities continues to undermine the efforts by governments to investigate, prosecute, and convict traffickers.

(6)   International Law Enforcement Academies should be more fully utilized in the effort to train law enforcement authorities, prosecutors, and members of the judiciary to address trafficking in persons-related crimes."

29 U.S.C. § 651. Occupational Safety and Health Act.

(a)   The Congress finds that personal injuries and illnesses arising out of work situations impose a substantial burden upon, and are a hindrance to, interstate commerce in terms of lost production, wage loss, medical expenses, and disability compensation payments.

(b)   The Congress declares it to be its purpose and policy, through the exercise of its powers to regulate commerce among the several States and with foreign nations and to provide for the general welfare, to assure so far as possible every working man and woman in the Nation safe and healthful working conditions and to preserve our human resources—

(1)   by encouraging employers and employees in their efforts to reduce the number of occupational safety and health hazards at their places of employment, and to stimulate employers and employees to institute new and to perfect existing programs for providing safe and healthful working conditions;

(2)   by providing that employers and employees have separate but dependent

responsibilities and rights with respect to achieving safe and healthful working conditions;

(3)   by authorizing the Secretary of Labor to set mandatory occupational safety and health standards applicable to businesses affecting interstate commerce, and by creating an Occupational Safety and Health Review Commission for carrying out adjudicatory functions under this chapter;

(4)   by building upon advances already made through employer and employee initiative for providing safe and healthful working conditions;

(5)   by providing for research in the field of occupational safety and health, including the psychological factors involved, and by developing innovative methods, techniques, and approaches for dealing with occupational safety and health problems;

(6)   by exploring ways to discover latent diseases, establishing causal connections between diseases and work in environmental conditions, and conducting other research relating to health problems, in recognition of the fact that occupational health standards present problems often different from those involved in occupational safety;

(7)   by providing medical criteria which will assure insofar as practicable that no employee will suffer diminished health, functional capacity, or life expectancy as a result of his work experience;

(8)   by providing for training programs to increase the number and competence of personnel engaged in the field of occupational safety and health;

(9)   by providing for the development and promulgation of occupational safety and health standards;

(10)   by providing an effective enforcement program which shall include a prohibition against giving advance notice of any inspection and sanctions for any individual violating this prohibition;

(11)   by encouraging the States to assume the fullest responsibility for the administration and enforcement of their occupational safety and health laws by providing grants to the States to assist in identifying their needs and responsibilities in the area of occupational safety and health, to develop plans in accordance with the provisions of this chapter, to improve the administration and enforcement of State occupational safety and health laws, and to conduct experimental and demonstration projects in connection therewith;

(12)   by providing for appropriate reporting procedures with respect to occupational safety and health which procedures will help achieve the objectives of this chapter and accurately describe the nature of the occupational safety and health problem;

(13)   by encouraging joint labor-management efforts to reduce injuries and disease arising out of employment.

Conclusion

Regardless of what services are needed, law enforcement agencies and community agencies have an obligation to assist the victim of this crime to reintegrate them back into mainstream society in a productive and healthy manner. Liaisons with other human services agencies can assure this seamless transition when participatory agencies plan together, accept the reality of the crime, recognize the crime, and work for the benefit of the victim.

Anyone can become a victim of human trafficking, although possible vulnerable populations include both legal and illegal immigrants, American children, and the poverty stricken.

It is important to emphasize that human trafficking and human smuggling are related but are not the same crime. Human trafficking is a crime against a person whereas human smuggling is a crime against a nation. These terms are not to be used interchangeably.

Since human trafficking is a market-based economy, traffickers are supporting the "supply and demand" theory. Nannies, maids, housekeepers, landscaping workers, nail salons, restaurants, industrial cleaning services, magazine salesperson, flowers/candy salesperson, agriculture worker, factory worker, boys choir, homeless drug-addicted man, Eastern European/Russian stripping or exotic dancing, Latino cantina bars, Korean room salons, hostess clubs, and other karaoke clubs, residential brothels based in homes, apartments, hotel/motel rooms, trailer parks, mobile trailers, escort services through bar/hotel based, internet based, private parties, boat cruises, strip clubs, phone chat lines, S&M

131

pornography rings, pimp-controlled prostitution-truck stops, street-based, internet/escort based, private parties or gang-based/motorcycle gangs could all be potential victims or house potential victims of human trafficking.

Author K. Bales quoted a Brazilian researcher in an article, saying that once a person's documents are confiscated, "the worker is dead as a citizen, and born as a slave." (Bales 2000) Research has given us the potential for humans to become victims of trafficking although the scope of the crime is still in question. Clearly, we need more definitive research to better understand the severity of the issue. The first step in combating this crime is recognizing the violation of our rights and securing a sound investigation and prosecution holding these traffickers responsible for their actions. Simultaneously, improvement is needed in the identification and prosecution of these cases. It is paramount that government and non-government resources work together to build partnerships prior to an incident occurring.

Public awareness, education and the establishment of protocols in all service agencies are crucial. Recommendations for awareness include training the general public, law enforcement, health providers, service providers, and other outreach services regarding immigrants, housing opportunities, victim compensation funds, and legal protections, as well as furthering research on the subject. Please join me in annually recognizing January 11th as National Human Trafficking Awareness Day.

Parents Need to Know

Research estimates that half of all runaways and/or missing children may be trafficked. Malls are ideal places for traffickers to find new victims. Red-flag indicators for possible human trafficking include being leery of older friends with flashy cars and a lot of money who provide a lot of attention to potential victims. The potential victim may be invited to go to a distant place, offered a modeling career, promised a good job, provided shopping sprees, and offered a free place to stay. Many times these offers are too good to be true.

Human trafficking is extremely damaging because, unlike drugs, these victims can be used over and over again; sometimes up to twenty times in a day/night. Once a drug is smoked, inhaled, injected, etc. it is gone. Victims of human trafficking are used repeatedly until they are no longer physically able to service another labor or sex act. The return on purchasing a human trafficking victim is incomprehensible. Consider the profits if you paid $5,000.00 for a female victim. It would not take long to re-coop your investment and begin to make a profit.

One out of every three teens on the street will turn to prostitution within forty-eight hours of running away from home. Predators will use Internet sites such as Face Book, Twitter, My Space, U-Tube, and Craigslist to lure vulnerable children. Parents need to closely monitor a child's computer involvement at all times. (Stop Trafficking Newsletter n.d.)

"Florencia Molina, enticed to Los Angeles by a woman from Mexico, was promised a job and free accommodations. 'I came to the United States with lots of dreams, but when I got here, my dreams were stolen,' said Molina, 33, whose three children stayed with her mother in Mexico until she could earn enough for their schooling. She was employed at a dress-maker's, sewing roughly 200 party dresses every 12 hours. Later, the shifts often stretched to 17 hours a day. Molina was locked in the shop at night--sleeping with a co-worker in a small storage room, without the option of showering or washing her clothes. The shop manager paid

Molina roughly $100 a week, confiscated her identity documents, and told her she would be arrested if she went to the authorities. Finally, she got permission to go to church, and there found a person who helped her get to the proper authorities." This is just one more example of a human trafficking situation. (Stop Trafficking Newsletter n.d.)

Another example of human trafficking involved Maria Suarez in California. "Today the balls and chains of slavery are often incognito. She came to California from Mexico seeking a job that would support her parents back home. In her search, she met a person on the street, who brought her to the home of an elderly man to do housework. Once inside the house, she was confined there for years, exploited, beaten and used. A locked door and messages of intimidation enslaved her." (Stop Trafficking Newsletter n.d.)

Unfortunately, U. S. citizens are supplying the demand for this crime. As long as there is a demand someone is going to feed the habit with the "supply," and human trafficking will continue. Author Moossy described a situation where "federal agents received a call from a worried parent who said his 13-year old daughter is engaging in commercial sex to earn money for a man she calls her boyfriend." It is up to the entire community, including parents of the children being victimized, to eliminate this adaptation of modern day slavery. (Moossy n.d.)

Cases of human trafficking are complex in nature and the needs of victim's need to be addressed immediately. Human trafficking is the deprivation of one's basic needs. The United States prides itself on the opportunity for life, liberty, and justice for all. Collectively we can protect this right by assuming a role in combating human trafficking in every community.

Appendix:
Victim Assistance Programs

Legal Aid of North Carolina, Battered Immigrant Project
(assists victims of sex trafficking throughout the state)
224 S. Dawson St
Raleigh, NC 27601
Coordinator (704) 971-2589
Attorney (919) 856-3196
http://www.legalaidnc.org/

Legal Aid of North Carolina, Farmworker Unit
(assists victims of labor trafficking throughout the state)
224 S. Dawson St
Raleigh, NC 27601
Director (919) 856-2180
Attorney (919) 856-2180
Client Line: 1-800-777-5869
http://www.legalaidnc.org/

Legal Services of Southern Piedmont, Immigrant Justice Project
(assists victims of Mecklenburg, Cabarrus, and Union counties)
1431 Elizabeth Avenue
Charlotte, NC 28204
Director (704) 971-2610
1-800-247-1931 Spanish intake line

Lutheran Family Services Carolinas
112 Cox Avenue
Raleigh, NC 27605
(919) 861-2806

North Carolina Coalition Against Domestic Violence
123 W. Main Street
Suite 700
Durham, NC 27701
(919) 956-9124
1-888-232-9124
http://www.nccadv.org/

North Carolina Coalition Against Sexual Assault
183 Wind Chime Court, Suite 100
Raleigh, NC 27615
(919) 870-8881
1-888-737-CASA
http://www.nccasa.org/

North Carolina Justice Center, Eastern Carolina Immigrant's Rights Project
224 S. Dawson St.
Raleigh, NC 27611
Attorney (919) 861-2072

North Carolina Justice Center, Immigrants Legal Assistance Project
(assists victims throughout the state)
224 S. Dawson St.
Raleigh, NC 27601
Director (919) 856-2185
Attorney (910) 856-3195

Polaris Project
P.O. Box 77892
Washington, DC 20013
(202) 745-1001
http://www.polarisproject.org/

Salvation Army
http://www.salvationarmy.org/

Triad Ladder of Hope
1022 Hutton Lane
Suite 106
High Point, NC 27262
(336) 883-2233 x223
http://www.triadladderofhope.org/

World Relief Refugee Services of North Carolina
2029 North Centennial Street
High Point, NC 27262
(336) 887-9007 or 1-800-535-5433
http://www.worldrelief.org

Bibliography

Anderson, Christopher. "Human Trafficking Instructor Package." Salemburg: North Carolina Justice Academy, January 2008.

Bales, K. In *Disposable People: New Slavery in the Global Economy.* Topeka Bindery, 2000.

Fisher, J. "Not for sale: Human trafficking." *International Association of Directors of Law Enforcement Standards and Training*, April 2009: 6-7.

Garrett, Ronnie. "Imprisoned in the american nightmare." *Law Enforcement Technology*, September 2008: 47.

"Human trafficking: A strategic framework could help enhance the interagency collaboration needed to effectively combat trafficking crimes." *United States Government Accountability Office.* 2007. http://www.gao.gov/new.items/d07915.pdf (accessed May 1, 2009).

Kyckelhahn T., Beck A., and Cohen T. "Characteristics of suspected human trafficking incidents, 2007-2008." Office of Justice Programs, U. S. Bureau of Justice, 2009.

Logan, T. K. and Hunt, G. "Understanding human trafficking in the United States." *Trauma, Violence and Abuse* 10, no. 1 (January 2009): 3-30.

Moossy, R. *Sex trafficking: Identifying cases and victims.* http://www.ojp.usdoj.gov/nij/journals/262/sex-trafficking.htm (accessed May 1, 2009).

North Carolina General Statutes. 2009. Address
Confidentiality Program.
http://www.ncga.state.nc.us/EnactedLegislation/Statutes/HTM
L/BySection/Chapter_15C/GS_15C-3.html (accessed May 1,
2009).

North Carolina General Statutes. 2009. Assistance for
program applicants.
http://www.ncga.state.nc.us/EnactedLegislation/Statutes/HTM
L/BySection/Chapter_15C/GS_15C-10.html (accessed May 1,
2009).

North Carolina General Statutes. 2009. Definitions.
http://www.ncga.state.nc.us/EnactedLegislation/Statutes/HTM
L/BySection/Chapter_15C/GS_15C-2.html (accessed May 1,
2009).

North Carolina General Statutes. 2009. Human trafficking.
http://www.ncga.state.nc.us/EnactedLegislation/Statutes/HTM
L/BySection/Chapter_14/GS_14-43.11.html (accessed May 1,
2009).

North Carolina General Statutes. 2009. Involuntary
servitude.
http://www.ncga.state.nc.us/EnactedLegislation/Statutes/HTM
L/BySection/Chapter_14/GS_14-43.12.html (accessed May 1,
2009).

North Carolina General Statutes. 2009. Purpose. Address
Confidentiality Program.
http://www.ncga.state.nc.us/EnactedLegislation/Statutes/HTM
L/BySection/Chapter_15C/GS_15C-1.html (accessed May 1,
2009).

North Carolina General Statutes. 2009. Responsibilities of the
District Attorney's Office.

http://www.ncga.state.nc.us/EnactedLegislation/Statutes/HTM
L/BySection/Chapter_15A/GS_15A-832.html (accessed May
1, 2009).

North Carolina General Statutes. 2009. Sexual servitude.
http://www.ncga.state.nc.us/EnactedLegislation/Statutes/HTM
L/BySection/Chapter_14/GS_14-43.13.html (accessed May 1,
2009).

Press, The Associated. "Mexican man sent to prison for sex
trafficking." *The News and Observer.* Washington, April 6,
2009.

Stop Trafficking Newsletter.
http://www.csasisters.org/pdfs/key_elements.pdf (accessed
April 20, 2009).

The Crime of Human Trafficking: A Law Enforcement Guide.
Directed by International Association of Chiefs of Police.
2006.

Trafficking Victims Protection Act. 2000.
http://www.state.gov/documents/organization/10492.pdf
(accessed April 28, 2009).

United States Department of Health and Human Services,
Administration for Children and Families, The Campaign to
Rescue and Restore Victims of Human Trafficking. *Child
Victims of Human Trafficking.* 2009.

United States Department of Health and Human Services,
Administration for Children and Families, The Campaign to
Rescue and Restore Victims of Human Trafficking. *Human
Trafficking Fact Sheet.* 2009.
United States Department of Health and Human Services,
Administration for Children and Families, The Campaign to

Rescue and Restore Victims of Human Trafficking. *Labor Trafficking Fact Sheet.* 2009.

United States Department of Health and Human Services, Administration for Children and Families, The Campaign to Rescue and Restore Victims of Human Trafficking. *Sex Trafficking Fact Sheet.* 2009.

United States Department of Justice, Federal Bureau of Investigation, and R.I.P.P.L.E. *"North Carolina Human Trafficking Task Force."*

United States Department of Justice, Office on Violence Against Women. "The Crime of Human Trafficking: A Law Enforcement Guide to Identification and Investigation."

United States Department of State. "Trafficking In Person Report." 2008.

Index

Printed in the United States of America.

Made in the USA
Monee, IL
15 July 2020